MISSOURI REAL PROPERTY TAX SALES

EXPLORING MISSOURI'S TAX SALE FRAMEWORK AND THE JONES-MUNGER ACT

SCOTT F. WALTERBACH, J.D.

mtss

missouri tax sale seminar, llc

Kansas City, MO
scott@mtss.llc • 816-601-1100
www.mtss.llc

Copyright © 2024 Scott F. Walterbach, J.D.

Printed in the United States of America.
ISBN: 978-1-63385-527-4

Published by
Word Association Publishers
205 Fifth Avenue
Tarentum, Pennsylvania 15084

www.wordassociation.com
1.800.827.7903

CONTENTS

CHAPTER 1

ABOUT the AUTHOR:
SCOTT WALTERBACH

Kindness to all, leaving things better than I found them, and brevity. I hope that's my legacy. I have two incredible, hardworking and fun-loving parents, and seven great siblings who taught me the important things in life. "Thank you" hardly seems adequate for the richness of my childhood.

I have a B.A. in Journalism from Truman State University, an M.P.A. in Urban Administration from the University of Missouri – Kansas City, and J.D. from the University of Indiana School of Law – Indianapolis.

After graduating law school in May 2007, I moved back to Kansas City, continued working, passed two bar exams, and renovated an old house.

I have a wonderful wife Katie, and four terrific children: Nash (10), Bo (8), Judd (7) and Hannah (5). They all remind me daily what is important and help me to have fun.

In late 2009, my best friend's father, who was a lawyer, was diagnosed with cancer. His firm called me and asked if I could lend a hand. Shortly thereafter, I made partner at Larry

Enkelmann, LLC. That work has evolved over the years, and in 2015 we changed the name to Bessine Walterbach, LLP.

Today I practice with three other attorneys and 14 staff in creditors' rights and tax sale foreclosures. It is fast paced, challenging, and fulfilling work. Our company's culture continues to evolve and improve.

I have been representing tax sale purchasers throughout Missouri since 2007, ranging from national organizations with large portfolios to individual buyers with a single property.

I've advised on all legal matters related to tax sales, and my firm files numerous tax sale quiet title lawsuits every year. I have handled tax sale cases in numerous state and federal trial courts, as well as appeals in tax sale cases in the Western District of Missouri, Eastern District of Missouri, the Missouri Supreme Court, and the 8th Circuit Court of Appeals.

I sat on a legislative panel in Jefferson City, MO to discuss needed changes to Missouri tax sale law in 2013. I am currently a legislative monitor for the National Tax Lien Association, and I am the founder of Missouri Tax Sale Seminar, LLC (est. Fall 2021).

Some of these achievements are born of hard work. But, I have had much help, for which I am grateful. Thank you to Matt Bessine, my friend and business partner, I value your perspective and work ethic. Thank you to my awesome employees, including my outstanding paralegal Felicia, who show up, apply themselves, and dare greatly every single day. Thank you to my family, my friends, and all the many supporters I have had, and continue to have, along the way. No person is an island, and my gratitude abounds.

For more information about Bessine Walterbach, LLP, visit www.bw-llp.com.

For more information on Missouri Tax Sale Seminar, visit www.mtss.llc.

Special thanks to Dr. Tom Costello, publisher at Word Association Publishers, and Ann Kayser, editor, for helping make this book the best it could be.

CHAPTER 2
LEGAL DISCLAIMER

This is intended for general educational purposes only. Though we are attorneys, we are not **your** attorneys. This is not legal advice. Legal advice would be to take general information and knowledge, combine it with current research, apply it to a given set of facts, and chart a course of action within a protected attorney-client privileged relationship. Any reader of this information agrees to hold Bessine Walterbach, LLP and its attorneys harmless and free from any and all liabilities, claims, losses, damages or obligations of any kind whatsoever, directly or indirectly related to this book. We are not your attorneys and do not represent you unless a written representation agreement is drafted by us, approved by you, and then counter-signed by us. Do not rely on this information, the risk is too great. Formally hire an attorney and get good legal advice before making or changing any decision, practice, or procedure. Good luck out there.

CHAPTER 3
INTRODUCTION

Missouri was first settled around 1735 – 1750. It was eventually named after a group of Sioux Indians known as Missouris, which translates to "wooden canoe people," a nod to their use of the area's navigable waterways. Missouri was admitted to the union August 10, 1821, as part of the Missouri Compromise, where Maine was admitted as free and Missouri was admitted without restrictions as to slavery. The Platte Purchase in the northwest in 1837 completed its current-day shape, where it ranks 21st in land mass among the fifty states. It is bordered by eight states, tied with Tennessee for the most in the U.S. (Those states are Kansas, Nebraska, Iowa, Illinois, Kentucky, Tennessee, Arkansas, and Oklahoma).

Today the Show-Me State's capitol sits overlooking the Missouri River in Jefferson City. As of the 2020 U.S. Census, Missouri's population is estimated at 6.154 million, ranking it 19th most populous in the country. Its largest cities are St. Louis to the east, Kansas City to the west, Springfield to the southwest, and Columbia in the center, in that order. Missouri's demographics at the 2020 census were approximately 77% white, 11.4% black, and no other race exceeded 5%. The 2022 median income was $53,547 annually for a single earner household. Missouri has a housing vacancy rate of 11.0%, just above the national 9.7% average.

This book focuses on R.S.Mo. Chapter 140, also known as the Jones-Munger Act, which governs most, but not all, Missouri tax sales[1], as described herein below. Missouri tax sales have been described as a deed state masquerading as a lien state, and I believe that to be an apt description. Tax sales are fundamentally a creature of statute. Said statutes are structured around, and overlaid by, concepts of constitutional due process. In this context, due process means notice and an opportunity to be heard before a taking of private property interests by state action.

Chapter 4 is a recapitulation of the statutes, best used for reference. It contains the title of every governing statute and in parentheses when it took effect or was last amended. Following each, in bold print, I have added my own description to help clarify what these statutes mean.

Starting with Chapter 5, I delve into particular areas of interest, including both particular statutory sections as well as the interplay of constitutional due process concepts and case law.

THE JONES-MUNGER ACT GOVERNS MOST, BUT NOT ALL, MISSOURI TAX SALES

Chapter 8 on statutory notice compliance and Chapter 15 on due process are particularly important in understanding the legal complexity of tax sales. Chapters 19 *et seq.* give updates on relatively recent developments.

---

1   R.S.Mo. Chapter 92 governs real estate tax foreclosures in St. Louis City. R.S.Mo. Chapter 141 governs real estate tax foreclosures in Jackson County. Both are judicial processes, as discussed subsequently herein.

Chapter 33 is about Missouri Tax Sale Seminar, LLC. I created this entity in 2021 to host an annual continuing legal education seminar in June of each year. Nothing like it existed in Missouri, and I finally decided to stop waiting for someone else to do it.

This book is not intended to be exhaustive or comprehensive regarding all aspects of Missouri tax sale law, but instead a starting point that begins a synthesis of a broad field. This is an effort to make a general understanding of the subject more accessible. Again, I caution against reliance: this is not legal advice, do not change what you do based on what you read here. At most, use it as a starting point for your own original research, or a conversation starter with an attorney who represents your interests regarding a particularized situation.

Taxes are one of the two proverbial certainties in life. The other is even less desirable. This is how Missouri deals with non-payment of real property taxes.

CHAPTER 4

BRIEF HISTORY OF JONES-MUNGER

Three sets of Missouri statutes govern delinquent real property tax collection: (1) the Missouri Municipal Land Reutilization Law, R.S.Mo. 92.700 et seq., providing a framework for judicial foreclosures but only applicable to St. Louis City[2]; (2) the Land Tax Collection Act, R.S.Mo. Chapter 141, providing also for judicial foreclosures but only applicable to Jackson County, Missouri; and (3) the Jones-Munger Act, R.S.Mo. Chapter 140, providing for administrative (non-judicial) foreclosure and applicable to all non-charter counties in Missouri. The former two involve a land tax lawsuit and a subsequent judicial confirmation of the sales. The latter, Chapter 140, is a non-judicial administrative process handled by each county collector. Chapter 140 is the focus of this book.

There are 114 counties in Missouri, 110 of which are "non-charter." St. Louis City and Jackson County (home to Kansas City) have charters and operate under separate rules as set forth above. Charter counties also include Clay,

---

2   St. Louis City is itself a separate "county" comprising the city proper. St. Louis County sits immediately adjacent to its west.

St. Charles, Jefferson, and St. Louis County. Though charter counties, all four of these counties have elected to operate under the provisions and requirements of the Jones-Munger Act, R.S.Mo. Chapter 140 for the collection of delinquent real property taxes. Clay County converted their collector from an elected to an appointed position with its new charter in 2020, but it does not appear (at least yet) that Clay will adopt a different method of real property tax foreclosure[3].

Jones-Munger was enacted in 1933, so Missouri has had the law for nearly half of its existence as a state. Prior to that time, Missouri tax liens were foreclosed judicially, having all interested parties named to a lawsuit (perhaps similar to the current version of R.S.Mo. Chapters 92 and 141). The state of Kansas utilizes a similar procedure.

Jones-Munger was a groundbreaking piece of legislation, radically changing the foundations of delinquent real property tax collection. *Schlafly v. Baumann*, 108 S.W.2d 363 (Mo. 1937). Rather than judicial foreclosure, for almost 100 years, most of Missouri has used administrative procedures to foreclose delinquent real property tax liens.

The Jones-Munger Act has been amended numerous times throughout its history. The legislature continues to address developments and tinker with the structure of the law to achieve the careful balancing of interests between collection of state revenue versus private property rights. Various subsections within the Jones-Munger Act

JONES-MUNGER RADICALLY CHANGED THE FOUNDATIONS OF DELINQUENT REAL PROPERTY TAX COLLECTION.

---

3   The Clay County Constitution is at: http://www.circuit7.net/documents/ publicmessage/Clay%20County%20Constitution%20-%20Final%20signed.pdf, dated 8/20/20, accessed 5/9/22.

have been changed recently, including amendments in 1996, 1998, 2000, 2003, 2004, 2005, 2010 (numerous changes including pre-tax sale notices), 2011, 2013 (numerous technical changes), 2015 (significant overhaul amendments addressing publication, subsequently due taxes, possession/trespass, shortening viability of certificate of purchase to 18 months, limiting disabled/minor redemption to five years from last taxes paid, limiting when costs can be reimbursed, and changes to 140.405 notices), 2018 (changes regarding surplusage), and 2019 (creating city of St. Joseph Land Bank).

The State Tax Commission of Missouri formerly had authority to construe and interpret Chapter 140 under R.S.Mo. § 140.660, but that legislative delegation of authority was repealed by Senate Bill 117 in 2011. Since that time, the state courts alone have decided Chapter 140 issues.

CHAPTER 5

THE STATUTES, AT-A-GLANCE WITH SYNOPSES

140.010 *County collector — enforcement of state's* lien. (8/28/1959) **If real property taxes are unpaid on January 1, delinquent and State has a lien.**

140.030 Collector to make delinquent lists. (8/28/1945) **A list is kept.**

140.040 Correction of delinquent lists by county commission — certified to whom. (8/28/1959) **County commission given an opportunity to make corrections.**

140.050 Clerk to make back tax book — delivery to collector, collection — ... (8/28/2013) **County Clerk keeps the back tax book.**

140.060 Back tax book — contents — interest. (8/28/1959) **Listed in numerical order with legal descriptions, name(s), years of delinquency, amount of taxes, interest and fees.**

140.070 Delinquent real estate taxes extended into back tax book. (8/28/2010) **Book includes all taxes due including those reported due by incorporated cities or towns.**

140.080 County clerk and collector, comparison of lists — clerk's certification. (8/28/2010) **They make sure the list is correct in the back tax book.**

140.090 Back tax book to be in alphabetical order. (8/28/1949) **When the assessor keeps the list in alphabetical, back tax book can be alphabetical instead of numerical as well.**

140.100 Penalty against delinquent lands — recording fee — additional recording ... (1/1/2018) **18% penalty except on redemptions prior to sale, 2% per month.**

140.110 Collection of back taxes, payments applied, how, exceptions — removal of lien. (8/28/2010) **Any interested person can redeem; payments always applied to oldest delinquency first.**

140.115 Lien prohibited on property in back tax book, when. (8/28/2013) **If disinterested party redeems, no lien without consent of owner.**

140.120 May compromise back taxes. (8/28/1959) **County Commission can compromise taxes upon finding that amount due exceeds the property's value.**

140.130 Examination of back tax books by board of equalization. (8/28/1945) **After 5 years delinquent, County board of equalization may, by majority, strike entry and cancel tax debt.**

140.140 Collector — reports. (8/28/1939) **Report all payments affecting back tax book.**

140.150 Lands, lots, mineral rights, and royalty interests subject to sale, when. (8/28/2013) **Collector mails notice to owner of any real estate (property, lot, mineral right, royalty interest, etc.) by regular mail then certified mail.**

140.160 Limitation of actions, exceptions — county auditor to annually audit. (8/28/2013) **Must administratively foreclose delinquent taxes within three years.**

140.170 County collector to publish delinquent land list — contents — site of sale ... (8/28/2015) **Fifteen days prior to the sale, list is published in newspaper; sale may be online.**

140.180 Lawful abbreviations. (8/28/1939) **For shortened property descriptions.**

140.190 Period of sale — manner of bids — prohibited sales — sale to nonresidents — restrictions, City of St. Joseph (8/28/2019) **Highest bid wins auction. Cannot owe other delinquent taxes and must sign affidavit to that effect. Nonresident bidders must appoint a local citizen for jurisdiction over disputes, title is issued in that person's name and then transferred to nonresident bidder.**

140.195 Entry on property not trespass, when. (8/28/2015) **No trespass if entry necessary to provide tax sale notice.**

140.220 County clerk to act as clerk of sale — fee. (8/28/2003) **Clerk records auction.**

140.230 Foreclosure sale surplus — deposited in treasury — escheats, when — proof ... (8/28/2018) **All surplusage tracked and paid to county treasury. Surplus priority is for lienholders first, then owners. Ninety day wait period after redemption expires, and proof of claims** must be provided by any applicant for prospective sur-plus payout. If no claim after three years, escheats to county school fund.

140.240 Second offering of delinquent lands and lots. (8/28/1959) **If not sold, offer again next year, same rules apply. Minimum bid is taxes due.**

140.250 Third offering of delinquent lands and lots, redemp-tion — subsequent sale — ... (8/28/2010) **Minimum bid is taxes due, but only 90-day redemption period as opposed to one year. Thereafter, collector only needs to offer once every five years, and post-third offerings have no minimum bid but you must pay subsequently due taxes.**

140.260 Purchase by county or city, when — procedure. (8/28/2010) **County or city may bid, with certain appli-cable provisions.**

140.270 Appointment of substitute or successor trustee — when and by whom. (8/28/1983) **Relates only to certain trustees under above section.**

140.280 Payment of total amount by purchaser — penalty for failure. (8/28/2003) **Full bid to be paid immediately, else 25% penalty to county school fund.**

140.290 Certificate of purchase — contents — fee — nonres-idents. (8/28/2013) **Property is not sold, purchaser buys certificate of purchase that memorializes the details of the sale. Assignable but with restrictions. Certificate is recorded in county land records. Provisions for non-resident bidders.**

140.300 Collector, written guaranty — action on — damages. (8/28/1959) **Collector warrants amount of taxes due,** and if not due because already paid, purchaser gets re-imbursed with interest.

140.310 Possession by purchaser, when — rents — rights of occupant and purchaser. (8/28/2015) **Immediate possession after one year on non-homesteads unless owner makes assignment of rents.**

140.320 Payment of taxes by purchaser — forfeiture. (8/28/1939) **Purchaser required to pay subsequently due taxes and not commit waste, else forfeit all rights.**

140.330 Suit to quiet title — duty of court where title invalid. (8/28/1939) **Name in the quiet title all publicly recorded interest holders and all others that may claim an interest. If the deed is invalid, the court ascertains the amount due for taxes plus interest not to exceed 10% to be paid within a reasonable time. If not paid, forever foreclosed. Rents and profits for not greater than seven years offered first, then the judgment debtor's full interest offered if previous offer is insufficient amount. If still insufficient, fee simple interest offered. General procedural rules apply.**

140.340 Redemption, when — manner. (8/28/2015) **Absolute right to redeem for the one year next ensuing. Right expires when purchaser acquires the deed or certificate expires. Redemption amount includes certain costs, fees, and interest not to exceed 10% on taxes plus 8% on subsequently due taxes. Costs incurred in sending notices are reimbursable if (1) incurred after March 1, (2) county is notified of the costs, and (3) collector views said costs as reasonable.**

140.350 Redemption by minors and incapacitated or disabled persons, when. (8/28/2015) **Redemption for minors/**

disabled persons extends to five years after date of last payment of taxes by the minor or disabled person.

140.360 Redemption — compensation for improvements — limitations. (8/28/2003) **If purchaser improved property after the one year, no redemption unless redemptioner pays or tenders value of improvements, to be determined in ejectment action if parties cannot agree on value.**

140.370 Redemption — record of sale. (8/28/2003) **Upon redemption, certificate of same is given to redemptioner and county clerk.**

140.380 Redemption by drainage, levee or improvement district — procedure. (8/28/1939) **Must redeem before foreclosing their lien, treated as assignment of the certificate of purchase to the district.**

140.405 Purchaser of property at delinquent land tax auction, deed issued to, when ... (8/28/2015) **KEY SECTION. Purchaser gets title search and sends notices to all publicly recorded interest holders at least 90 days prior to being authorized to acquire the deed. Last known address by certified and regular mail. Presumed delivered if certified mail returned signed, regular mail not returned, regular mail returned "refused." If certified mail returned unsigned and regular mail returned for reason other than refusal, purchaser must attempt additional notice efforts. Purchaser notifies collector by affidavit with copies of all notices and envelopes sent. When said notice provided, purchaser authorized to acquire deed (must be after one year). Authorized defined to mean complied with notice requirements to satisfaction of collector, paid required fees, produced original** certificate of purchase, and paid all subsequently due taxes. **Failure to comply results in loss of all interest in real estate *except* lien may remain under 140.550 or 570.** Any owner or interest holder must first redeem before transferring or encumbering their interest. At a third offering, any publicly recorded interests must be notified within 45 days, giving 90 days to redeem. Provisions for notifying parties abroad.

140.410 Execution and record of deed by purchaser — failure — assignment ... (8/28/2015) **Purchaser must pay all subsequently due taxes and get the deed within 18 months of the sale.**

140.420 Deed to purchaser if unredeemed. (8/28/2015) **If not redeemed, collector's deed "shall vest in the grantee an absolute estate in fee simple" subject to subsequently due taxes, which are never extinguished.**

140.430 Deed to heirs in case of purchaser's death. (8/28/1939) **Self-explanatory.**

140.440 Payment of taxes by holder of purchase certificate — subsequent certificate. (8/28/2003) **Must pay subsequently due taxes, provisions for handling of any surplus.**

140.450 Cancellation and filing of certificate — proof of loss. (8/28/1939) **What happens when an original certificate of purchase is lost.**

140.460 Execution of conveyance — form. (8/28/2013) **Gives form language for collector's deed with no title warranties. *Prima facie* evidence of regularity of all proceedings and valid title in grantee.**

140.470 Variations from form. (8/28/2013) **Collector makes any needed changes.**

140.480 Record of land sold kept by collector. (8/28/1939) **Collector keeps records.**

140.490 Action by damaged party against collector. (8/28/1939) **Can sue collector for actual damages if you actually paid taxes and were not given credit, plus 10% penalty.**

140.500 Mistake in name not to invalidate sale. (8/28/1939) **Wrong owner name of no effect.**

140.510 Form not to affect validity — presumption of validity. (8/28/1939) **Substance over form, a technicality doesn't absolve liability for tax.**

140.520 Irregularity and omissions not to invalidate proceedings. (8/28/1939) **Non-substantive irregularities do not invalidate proceedings.**

140.530 Invalidity of sale, when. (8/28/1939) **What <u>does</u> invalidate a sale are things that go right to the heart of tax collection: land not liable in the first place, taxes were actually paid prior to the sale, legal description failed to identify lot sold with reasonable certainty.**

140.540 Invalidity of sale — refund of purchase money — tolling of statute. (8/28/1939) **Prior to issuing a deed, when an error is caught, collector can refund purchaser.**

140.550 Transfer of lien in case of invalid deed. (8/28/1939) **When such an error is caught, purchaser retains a lien to protect the investment; no windfall to owner.**

140.560 Release of lien by holder upon payment. (8/28/1939) **Relates to above section.**

140.570 Lien in full force in certain cases when conveyance is invalid. (8/28/1939) **If deed invalidated for nearly any reason, lien of purchaser continues and land still responsible for taxes paid. Court ascertains correct** amount and orders it paid, else foreclosed just like 140.330.

140.580 Action for the recovery of possession. (8/28/1939) **Can sue for possession whether taken yet or not.**

140.590 Suits against purchaser of tax lands to be brought within three years. (8/28/1983) **Collector's deed must be challenged within three years of recording unless minor/disabled.**

140.600 Suit to set aside tax deeds — actual tender not necessary. (8/28/1939) **Any challenger to a collector's deed must tender refund to tax sale purchaser of taxes paid plus interest and fees. Actual tender not necessary, just plead the offer. If the challenger prevails, the court then ascertains and orders lien in that amount.**

140.610 Proof by claimant of invalidity of sale. (8/28/1939) **Valid defenses, other than due process, limited to land not subject to tax, taxes paid prior, taxes redeemed prior.**

140.620 County records, *prima facie* evidence — moneys paid to successor. (8/28/1939) **Certified records as set forth above are *prima facie* evidence of issuance of certificate and any redemption.**

140.630 Defendant may make claim for taxes paid — not to affect other defenses. (8/28/1949) **Allows purchaser to plead the amount under 140.600 without prejudice to defending the case otherwise.**

140.640 Personal judgments not authorized. (8/28/1939) **No personal judgments for real estate taxes or interest due to a taxing jurisdiction like a county, drainage or levee district, or a city.**

140.665 Law applies to counties and cities and certain officers. (8/28/2013) **Broadens definition of "collector" herein to include like positions with different titles.**

140.670 City delinquent taxes, when returned — duties of collector. (8/28/1959) **Cities shall report delinquent lists to county by March to be included in sale.**

140.680 Power to collect such taxes. (8/28/1939) **County has power to collect city taxes so reported.**

140.690 Such taxes a lien. (8/28/1959) **Lien for city taxes same as for state tax under 140.010.**

140.710 To be embodied in list with state and county taxes. (8/28/1939) **City taxes and assessments so reported kept in same list but in different column.**

140.720 Collector to furnish statement to city — fees. (8/28/1945) **Collector reports to city treasurers same as they report to county clerk.**

140.722 Conveyances subject to covenants and easements. (8/28/1996) **Collector's deeds are always subject to valid recorded covenants running with the land, valid easements of record and valid easements in use, which are not extinguished.**

End of real property tax section of Chapter 140. After this begins the personal property tax and general collection section, 140.730 - 855. Sections 140.980 through 140.1015 contain provisions for the City of St. Joseph Land Bank, which exceeds the scope of this book.

CHAPTER 6
PROCEDURAL OVERVIEW & NUANCES

The Jones-Munger Act is at Revised Statutes of Missouri (R.S.Mo.) Chapter 140, available at www.revisor.mo.gov. It provides for an annual sale, conducted by the county collector, of the State's delinquent super-priority tax liens, occurring at 10:00 a.m. on the fourth Monday in August of each year in every county. §§ 140.010, 140.150.1. Bidders must be present, unless the sale is online – Clay County was first to do this in 2018. Others, like St. Louis County, followed suit as part of a response to the COVID-19 pandemic. A 2022 amendment to R.S.Mo. §§ 140.170.3 and 140.190.2 makes explicit the availability of online auctions.

Collectors have some discretion regarding exactly how "delinquent" the taxes must be before being put on the tax sale for a first offering. All taxes are delinquent on January 1 of the year following assessment, with penalties and interest accruing thereon. The first offering of a tax lien can be made in August, after approximately nine months of delinquency. Alternatively, the first offering could be the following August, when delinquency has persisted for about a year and nine months. Tax sales must occur within three years of the initial delinquency, else no proceedings for enforcement of the State's lien are valid. § 140.160.

Prior to the tax lien sale, the collector mails two notices to the owner of record, regular and then certified. The collector records all delinquencies in the back tax book and publishes notice, of each lien to be sold, for three consecutive weeks in a local newspaper of general circulation in the county. § 140.170.1. This publication is required by the Missouri Constitution, Article X Section 1:

> Section 13. Tax sales—limitations—contents of notices.—No real property shall be sold for state, county or city taxes without judicial proceedings, unless the notice of sale shall contain the names of all record owners thereof, or the names of all owners appearing on the land tax book, and all other information required by law.

This is the only mention of tax sales in the Missouri Constitution.

At a Chapter 140 sale only a lien is sold, not the property itself. The minimum bid must be for the taxes due (plus all applicable interest and penalties), and if no bidder offers the same, the lien would remain in the back tax book to be offered again the following August. § 140.240.1. A second offering is functionally the same as a first.

For policy reasons, third offerings are treated differently: there is still a minimum bid of taxes due, but only a 90-day statutorily required redemption period. § 140.250. Post-third offerings have no minimum bid and no statutory redemption period at all, but the government has protection because taxing jurisdictions, via a trustee, can themselves bid on the lien.

§ 140.260. Yet due process still applies. Even if the statutes do not require notice, the state and federal constitutions do. *See* Chapter 15. Third and post-third offerings are generally undesirable properties, and not the focus herein, except to say they have the same constitutional concerns about notice.

A prospective Chapter 140 investor must meet certain qualifications to bid, else a sale "may" be invalidated. For example, the bidder must not owe delinquent taxes in the county. § 140.190.2. The successful bidder does not purchase property at the sale, but instead buys the State's lien interest, for which they are issued a certificate. § 140.290.1. The certificate purchaser then "steps into the shoes" of the State's lien position, and he or she assumes the statutory (§ 140.405) and constitutional (due process) notice obligations, both of which must fully be completed before effectuating a lawful "taking" of private property by state action (when the collector's deed is recorded).

THE BIDDER MUST NOT OWE DELINQUENT TAXES IN THE COUNTY

The lien of the State so sold is represented by a tax sale certificate, which recites the details of the sale and is recorded in county land records. Each certificate bears simple interest at a rate not to exceed ten percent per annum (10%) on the taxes paid; there is no interest on any excess bid amount; and interest not to exceed eight percent per annum (8%) on any taxes subsequently to come due and paid by the tax sale purchaser. §§ 140.290.2, 140.340.2. Interest may continue beyond one year, but it ceases to accrue when a county collector notifies a purchaser of a redemption. § 140.340.4.

During the one-year period next ensuing, every owner, occupant, lienholder or any other interested person has an absolute right to redeem the property from the first or second offering sale. Redemption is accomplished by paying to the county collector the taxes previously paid by the tax sale purchaser, plus the interest due thereon, and any penalties that are reasonable and customary costs of sale. § 140.340.1. A redemption means all lienholder priorities continue as they were prior to the sale. A redemption also means the tax sale purchaser is notified, and turns in their certificate, at which time they are reimbursed the taxes paid plus interest. § 140.340. They also get their surplus back but without interest.

Sophisticated bidders, therefore, when exceeding the amount of taxes due in a competitive auction, are calculating the total investment and its effective interest rate to see if the ROI (return on investment) makes sense for them. Some bidders are keen on the interest; others are in it for REO (real estate owned). Most, but not all, properties redeem. Many redeem in the last few days prior to the one-year anniversary of the sale. I have never tracked the numbers or been given any studies on it, but my intuition is that perhaps 80% or more are redeemed within the allowed time.

Throughout the redemption period, the tax sale purchaser "is vested with an inchoate or inceptive interest in the land …." *M & P Enterprises, Inc. v. Transamerica Financial Services*, 944 S.W.2d 154, 157 (Mo. banc 1997) *quoting State ex rel. Baumann v. Marburger*, 182 S.W.2d 163, 165 (Mo. 1944). Missouri cases have not directly addressed whether this is a real property interest or a general intangible, which is relevant to how tax sale certificates may be secured or encumbered. I have treated the tax certificate as an interest in real property, but I have not received any challenge to that assertion.

Tax sale purchasers must meet the notice requirements established in R.S.Mo. § 140.405, else they lose their *ownership* interest (no longer *all* interest) in the property and may be relegated to a lien status for the taxes paid. § 140.405.8, pursuant to §§ 140.405.8, 140.550, and 140.570 (2015). "At least ninety days prior to the date the purchaser is authorized to acquire the deed" as defined by § 140.405.9, the purchaser was required to notify the former owner(s) and all publicly recorded lienholders of their right to redeem, by both certified and regular mail. § 140.405.2; *and see Harpagon MO, LLC v. Bosch*, 370 S.W.3d 579 (Mo. 2012); *legislatively abrogated, A.L. 2015 H.B. 613.* The sender keeps a clear record of everything sent and everything returned by the US Postal Service, to submit its affidavit verifying compliance with §§ 140.405.2 and 140.405.5. The collector now has discretion to deny such a deed application under § 140.405.9.

The Jones-Munger Act acknowledges the reality that many tax sale houses are vacant or abandoned by giving rebuttable presumptions of notice receipt. § 140.405.2.

If no interested party redeems, the purchaser produces the certificate along with an affidavit and other required attachments, after the one-year period but before the certificate expires upon eighteen months after the sale. §§ 140.410, 140.405. After verifying statutory compliance, the collector issues and records its collector's deed for taxes, which vests in the purchaser an absolute estate in fee simple subject to (1) subsequent taxes due, (2) valid recorded covenants running with the land, (3) easements of record and (4) easements in use. §§ 140.420, 140.722.

Tax sales may also be subject to other liens given elevated priority by statutes outside of Chapter 140. My research indicates these may include, but are not necessarily limited to, the following:

1. R.S.Mo. § 67.399.4 – Abatement of Public Nuisance registration fees set by municipal ordinances.

2. R.S.Mo. § 67.469 – Neighborhood Improvement District liens, taxes and assessments.

3. R.S.Mo. § 67.1521.5 – Community Improvement District liens, taxes and assessments.

4. R.S.Mo. § 67.2815.5 – Property Assessment for Clean Energy liens, taxes and assessments.

5. R.S.Mo. § 80.430 – taxes due a Village or Town.

6. R.S.Mo. § 88.897 – sidewalk improvement costs in cities of 30,000 or less (stating a first and prior tax lien, but also providing the same is secondary to state taxes).

7. R.S.Mo. § 94.160 – taxes due Third Class Cities.

8. R.S.Mo. § 94.190.4 – Fourth Class City assessments, but provides superior to all liens except state taxes, so may not be applicable.

9. R.S.Mo. § 94.310 – taxes due Fourth Class Cities.

10. R.S.Mo. § 137.085.2 – Assessment and taxation of government lands.

11. R.S.Mo. § 139.070 – providing a lien for mortgagees who pay current taxes, to be collected as part of the taxes currently due.

12. R.S.Mo. § 151.210 – Railroad company or street railroad company taxes, but enforcement is by lawsuit under § 151.230, so possibly not applicable.

13. R.S.Mo. §§ 238.232.3 & 238.233.1 – Transportation Development District liens, taxes and assessments.

14. R.S.Mo. § 243.370.1 – Drainage District liens, taxes and assessments.

15. R.S.Mo. §§ 245.175.3, 245.205, 245.215, 245.220, and 245.445 – Levee District liens, taxes and assessments.

16. R.S.Mo. § 247.500 – Metropolitan Water Supply District liens, taxes and assessments.

17. R.S.Mo. §§ 249.255, 249.640.2 and 249.645.3 – Sewer District liens, taxes and assessments.

18. R.S.Mo. § 256.320.2 – Missouri Water Development Fund debts.

19. R.S.Mo. § 263.456.3 – Noxious Weed Control Area liens, taxes and assessments.

20. R.S.Mo. § 271.230 – Stray Animal fines, liens, taxes and assessments.

21. R.S.Mo. § 278.250.6 – Watershed District liens, taxes and assessments.

22. R.S.Mo. § 321.270.2 – Fire Protection District liens, taxes and assessments.

If these types of issues are revealed in a title search report, a prudent tax sale investor would want to further research the same and learn, to the extent possible, its effect on the foreclosure process. If one of these interests survives the tax sale, it is better to know that up front so a prudent investment decision can be made.

CHAPTER 7
GENERAL STATUTORY COMPLIANCE

Every county collector conducts their sale a little differently, so it is important to ensure all local requirements are met by working closely with the collector. Some requirements are different due to local customs, differing interpretations of applicable statutes and/or cases, or due to the size and scope of the county's population and their tax sale. For example, rural county sales look much different than sales in counties that are more urban. Information can typically be found on the collector's web site, but not for every county.

A tax sale purchaser should complete everything required to register by working with the collector. Certain affidavits and registration paperwork prior to the date of the auction are typical. A prospective purchaser must file an affidavit of non-delinquency on other real estate taxes. If the bidder is a corporation, a written designation of the individual bidder may be required. As a business matter, you would want to receive a copy of the delinquency list and begin due diligence on available properties prior to the sale.

A foreign person or entity (residing outside the state) rightfully should be wary of their ability to bid at all, due to imprecise language in the statute. § 140.190.2. But assuming that hurdle in statutory interpretation could be cleared in the face of a challenge, such a bidder would want to make sure the proper appointment of a resident agent was timely and properly made. § 140.190.2. The resident bidder transfers the property to them after the deed is recorded in the resident bidder's name.

These additional nonresident requirements do not apply to a domestic Missouri corporation, whether a corporation, limited liability company, or partnership. Jurisdictional concerns are absent when such an entity maintains a registered agent within the state for purposes of service of process.

ADDITIONAL NONRESIDENT REQUIREMENTS DO NOT APPLY TO A DOMESTIC MISSOURI CORPORATION

A collector's deed is *prima facie* evidence of the regularity of all proceedings, including notices, and of valid title passed. The date of recording is the operative date of transfer, which can dictate when the tax sale purchaser becomes responsible for bills, assessments, premises liability risk, casualty, etc. regarding the property.

Allowed defenses are limited as set forth below. Former owners and lienholders who challenge the sale seem to enjoy the "kitchen sink" defense approach, complaining about every hyper-technical, inconsequential aspect of the tax sale. These are not meritorious defenses by law, but they can influence the backstory of a case and make things more difficult. Missouri law disfavors takings and judges seem inclined to set aside collector's deeds. A prudent purchaser dots the "i"s and crosses the "t"s in its sale preparations, preparing for such a foreseeable challenge.

The burden of proof at trial, if litigated properly, ought to be on the tax sale challenger to come forward with admissible evidence demonstrating invalidity of the sale or the deed. § 140.460.2; *Trailwoods Homeowners Assoc. v. Scott*, 938 S.W.2d 669 (Mo. App. E.D. 1997). This dynamic can, and perhaps should, affect every pleading, motion, procedure and trial preparation in a Missouri tax sale quiet title case.

CHAPTER 8
STATUTORY NOTICE COMPLIANCE

Courts have interpreted the prima facie validity of prior proceedings as including *prima facie* validity of notices. *Stadium West Properties v. Johnson*, 133 S.W.3d 128, 136 (Mo. App. W.D. 2004); *Mitchell v. Atherton*, 563 S.W.3d 13 (Mo. banc 1978).

As discussed elsewhere in this book, § 140.405 requirements are overlaid by constitutional due process concepts. Compliance with both is key. Statutory compliance and due process compliance are parallel tracks: separate legal concepts but operating simultaneously in every tax sale case. Therefore this Chapter cannot be read in isolation, but must be considered in concert with Chapter 15.

Before one can move to the more complex or perhaps fuzzier due process concepts, the focus initially should be on compliance with the current black-letter requirements of § 140.405. The presumption of regularity, after all, is rebuttable.

First, timing is important. Most tax sale purchasers want to recover their costs for (1) the title search report, and (2) postage for mailing. These costs are recoverable as part of a subsequent redemption only if those costs are incurred after

March 1 following the sale. The collector has discretion to evaluate "reasonable and customary" costs of the title search report and the mailing of notices. Collectors will not approve inflated costs. Unreasonably high costs are an artificial barrier to redemption and therefore an unconstitutional taking. It is a serious issue.

The tax sale is at the end of August. Essentially nothing else happens until March 1 of the following calendar year, except perhaps a redemption. § 140.340.2.

Next, we turn to § 140.405. A title search report is procured from a licensed title company. The purchaser shall notify all publicly recorded interest holders of their right to redeem. Notices are sent by first class and certified mail, copies of the notices and all envelopes kept. Notices must be sent to the "last known available address," which entails reasonable efforts consistent with constitutional due process. *Bullard v. Holt*, 158 S.W.3d 868, 871 (Mo. App. S.D. 2005).

THE PURCHASER SHALL NOTIFY ALL PUBLICLY RECORDED INTEREST HOLDERS OF THEIR RIGHT TO REDEEM.

If the presumptions of delivery are rebutted as provided in § 140.405.2, additional notice attempts or efforts must be taken and documented for the eventual deed application. The statute is silent on what additional attempts are sufficient.

The subject property must be accurately described in the notice of the right to redeem, as well as the collector's published notice and the collector's deed itself. All three should be consistent. The standard is reasonable certainty, not perfection, and extrinsic evidence is permissible. *See generally Stadium W. Props., LLC v. Johnson*, 133 S.W.3d 128 (Mo. App.

W.D. 2004); *Wayward, Inc. v. Shafer*, 936 S.W.2d 843 (Mo. App. E.D. 1996); *Podlesak v. Wesley*, 849 S.W.2d 728 (Mo. App. S.D. 1993) (sufficiency of legal description is a question of fact for trial).

The language of the notice must be carefully crafted, both for statutory and due process compliance. There is no silver bullet that all attorneys agree upon but there have been lessons over the years of what not to do. Courts have reached differing conclusions as to the time component to be stated and the "forever barred and foreclosed" language. *United Asset Mgmt. Trust Co. v. Clark*, 332 S.W.3d 159 (Mo. App. W.D. 2010); *Ndegwa v. KSSO, LLC*, ED 968315, 2011 WL 4790633 (Mo. App. E.D. 2011); *Valli v. Glasgow Enterpr., Inc.*, 204 S.W.3d 273 (Mo. App. E.D. 2006); *Keylien Corp. v. Johnson*, 284 S.W.3d 606 (Mo. App. E.D. 2009). *See* Chapter 15. I also propose a statutory "safe harbor" for simplicity and consistency in notice language. At this time, that proposal does not seem to be a legislative priority.

CHAPTER 9
TYPES of CLAIMANTS

Often the "owner" of a property is not the only one with a legal interest in it. Think of a regular house in the suburbs. There are probably utility easements from several different companies or municipalities, at a minimum. But when a property is tax-delinquent, the taxpayer might not have paid other creditors as well. That might include federal taxes, state taxes, mortgages, homeowner's associations, utility companies, or other judgment creditors. All of these claimants may have a lien (an interest) in the property.

A tax sale purchaser learns of parties with these types of claims by ordering a title search report from a licensed attorney or licensed title company as discussed elsewhere in this book. Many types of claimants are straightforward, such as a co-owner, a spouse, a beneficiary deed grantee, an assignee of rents, or a homeowner's association lien. Others are less apparent as to who gets notice, where to send it, and what effect the notice has.

Missouri uses deeds of trust for mortgage purposes because foreclosures are non-judicial and therefore more efficient and cost-effective. There are three parties to a standard deed of trust: (1) the homeowner/grantor/mortgagor, (2) the trustee, and (3) the lender/grantee/mortgagee. A deed of trust creates a lien and nothing more. *JD Wealth LLC v. U.S. Bank National Association ND, et al.*, ED111572 (12/19/23) (regional reporter citation not yet available).

Failure to send notice to the deed of trust beneficiary has invalidated a sale. *Glasgow Enterpr., Inc. v. Kusher,* 231 S.W.3d 201 (Mo. App. E.D. 2007). One case seemed to indicate the trustee on a deed of trust was entitled to notice. *Cedarbridge v. Eason*, 293 S.W.3d 462 (Mo. App. E.D. 2009) (all parties appearing on the first page of a deed of trust are entitled to notice, where the tax sale purchaser failed to send notice to any party). However, *JD Wealth* distinguished *Cedarbridge* in holding that the trustee was not the "holder" of a redeemable interest and therefore was not entitled to notice where the tax sale purchaser sent notice to the lender but not the trustee. *Id. at 14. JD Wealth* also distinguished *Glasgow Enterpr., Inc. v. Kusher,* 231 S.W.3d 201 (Mo. App. E.D. 2007), where the tax sale purchaser sent notice of the right to redeem to the trustee but not the lender. *JD Wealth's* utility in future cases may be limited as very fact-specific, but it should be consulted in understanding notices of the right to redeem to the parties involved in a deed of trust.

Mortgage Electronic Registration Systems, Inc. ("MERS") is an entity that cleverly created a back-channel way for mortgagees to sell mortgage paper without always having to record new information with the county. They are often listed as the deed of trust beneficiary's "nominee". When appearing in public records, it is best to send them notice, as that seems to be one of the primary purposes of their existence since 1993. Court cases have been mixed about what MERS proper role is, in various contexts. But failure to send notice to MERS could give a deed of trust beneficiary a due process defense, if they were set up to receive notice through MERS alone (as opposed to public record). See *MERS, Inc. v. Bellistri*, 2010 WL 2720802 (Mo. App. E.D. 2010); *but see Bellistri v. Ocwen Loan Servicing, LLC*, 284 S.W.3d 619 (Mo. App. E.D. 2009) (finding a failed assignment from MERS to Ocwen, depriving Ocwen of standing).

If the Federal Deposit Insurance Corporation (FDIC) is a receiver of a lender also showing as a deed of trust beneficiary, there is a split of authority as to whether such an interest is extinguished in a tax sale. *37 Huntington St., H, LLC v. City of Hartford*, 772 A.2d 633 (Conn. App. Ct. 2001) (allows extinguishment); *PLM Tax Cert. Prog. 1991-92, LP v. Denton Invs. Inc.*, 986 P.2d 243 (Ariz. Ct. App. 1999) (disallows extinguishment).

The Internal Revenue Service sometimes has recorded liens against former owners of tax-distressed properties. Said liens may be foreclosed as other liens, but only with highly particularized notices, and perhaps longer periods of redemption, pursuant to IRS Publication 786 and 4235 and other applicable federal law. If the IRS is in your title search, consult a knowledgeable attorney to assist in proper noticing.

Judgment creditors of former owners do not always appear in a title search, especially if the former owner has a common name. A separate search of court records may be necessary to find such parties. Mechanic's lien holders are the same – they may not appear in a title search, such that a separate search of certain court or other county records may be necessary to find their recorded interest.

Municipal neighborhood improvement district (NID) assessments may also pose a problem.

Notice to the city or other entity making the assessment and recording the delinquency as a lien on the property is necessary. There remains some question about extinguishing such an assessment in a Chapter 140 sale. Past installments due on the assessment are collected just as other city taxes and have equal priority as taxes. As to future installments due on the assessment up on the property, those may be extinguished if the city fails to accelerate and report the full balance due at the time of the tax sale. See the following cases where the tax sale purchaser prevailed at the trial court level on this issue, and appeals were later dismissed. *WMAC 2014, LLC v. Suncrest Investment Property Service, LLC, et al.*, 15CY-CV07931 and 15CY-CV07935.

As to <u>Community</u> Improvement Districts (CIDs), tax sales may not extinguish such a district's lien for past assessments because the CID statute provides the CID lien is perpetual. *See Real Estate Recovery, LLC v. Branson Hills Facility Infrastructure CID*, SD36349 (10/14/20). Transportation development districts ("TDDs") may be entitled to notice as well, and their interests and future assessments may survive.

Municipal special "tax" bills are not of equal priority with general county *ad valorem* taxes. *State ex rel. Land v. Trimble*, 2 S.W.2d 616 (Mo. banc 1928); *accord* 64A C.J.S. *Municipal Corporations*, § 1809.c (1999). Some originating statutes of particular special tax bills are not clear as to priority in relation to general taxes. *E.g.*, § 71.285 and § 67.398. Taxes are for general government purposes, benefit the entirety or most of the governed, and are irrespective of a specific cost incurred. Fees and special assessments, by contrast, are done for a specific purpose, serving a geographically concentrated area, and the cost determines the amount charged. For a thorough discussion of the difference between taxes, fees and special assessments, see *Zahner v. City of Perryville*, 813 S.W.2d 855 (Mo. banc 1991). Generally speaking, taxes survive but other charges and assessments do not (even if they are clumsily titled a "special tax bill," which are typically mere assessments). At any rate, a valid defense to a city's attempted enforcement of such a lien could be the five-year statute of limitations under R.S.Mo. § 516.120.

A PACE lien holder under R.S.Mo. § 67.2800 et seq. also may pose an issue for a tax sale purchaser. PACE stands for Property Assessed Clean Energy Financing. This program is conducted by a board which is a political subdivision of the state, for the purpose of financing renewable energy improvements (mostly solar panels, but perhaps a variety of other types). The financing enables the homeowner to pay off the cost of renewable energy improvements over a twenty-year assessment on their tax bill. Such an assessment is subject to Department of Energy guidelines, which include notice to an existing mortgagee. A tax sale purchaser would want to work closely with a knowledgeable attorney if a PACE lien arises in a title search.

Certain drainage or levee districts may have liens that have equal priority with taxes. See § 249.645.3 (8/28/1999). If a drainage or levee district lien appears in a title search report, counsel should be consulted on how to properly notify said entity and what effect the same would have on title passed by the collector's deed.

A minor, disabled or incapacitated person has an extended period of redemption. Incapacity or disability is defined as including total or partial inability to communicate decisions or manage personal financial resources. *See* R.S.Mo. § 475.010(6) and (11). The non-payment of a fundamental tax obligation is likely self-proving of the issue, but even if not, the evidentiary bar is exceedingly low.

Formerly the period could have been infinite, as it extended until the end of the disability under R.S.Mo. § 140.350, but the same was amended in 2015. The legislature evidently deemed such uncertainty undesirable and put an outer limit on their right to redeem. Now, any such minor, disabled or incapacitated person may redeem at any time within five years of the last date taxes were paid on the property by the taxpayer or their predecessor or representative. A tax sale purchaser may not know if the person is a minor or is disabled, but should be aware of this possibility, and any due process implications.

If a notice recipient is on active military duty with the United States military or one of its allies, they may have certain protections under the Servicemembers Civil Relief Act, 50 U.S.C. § 3901 et seq.

If notice must be sent to someone in a foreign country, a tax sale purchaser would want to have their attorney carefully review, and comply with, § 140.405.10, which was added to the statute in the 2015 amendments.

Unknown possessors of the property, such as residents, tenants or occupants, may argue entitlement to notice via due process, even without a recorded interest that would entitle them to a statutory notice. Prudence dictates always sending notice to possessors, especially if known. The same goes for spouses or former spouses without publicly recorded interests, especially if a deed of trust or other document in the chain of title refers to a spouse without a death recital otherwise appearing.

A tax sale purchaser may be well-advised to review probate records carefully to determine heirs of public record, if a former owner or lien holder is deceased.

CHAPTER 10
EFFECT OF REDEMPTION

Redemption means paying the taxes after the tax sale certificate is sold. A redemption clears the tax debt, and in so doing the parties with an interest in the land regain the status quo as it existed immediately prior to the sale.

Owners and lienholders can redeem by paying the taxes, interest, costs of sale, penalties and fees due on the property to the collector. The redemption payment must be made prior to the the tax sale purchaser's interest being perfected, which period is, at a minimum, one year (more detail below).

When an owner or lienholder pays the redemption amount to the collector, the collector then notifies the tax sale purchaser of the redemption and requests the tax sale purchaser return their certificate.

When the certificate is submitted, the redemption amount is paid back to the purchaser. Generally, this includes taxes plus 10% interest, subsequently due taxes plus 8% interest, plus reasonable costs of sale.

The surplus, if any, also is returned to the purchaser. However, surplus does not accrue interest in the interim. Redemption is not a negotiation between the tax sale purchaser and any homeowner or lienholder. There is nothing a tax sale purchaser could or should do to create any artificial barriers to the right to redeem.

The time for redemption, from a first or second offering, is a minimum of one year but could be as long as eighteen months, depending on when the purchaser is authorized to acquire the deed. § 140.405.9. There is a question as to whether a stranger to the title may redeem under § 140.340.1, which limits redemption to the owner, lienholder or occupant. However, it is clear any such stranger may not take a lien against the property to secure repayment from the owner, without the knowledge and consent of the owner. § 140.115.

THE TIME FOR REDEMPTION, FROM A FIRST OR SECOND OFFERING, IS A MINIMUM OF ONE YEAR

For a general discussion of the right of redemption, see *Hobson v. Elmer*, 163 S.W.2d 1020 (Mo. 1942) and *Wetmore v. Berger*, 188 S.W.2d 949 (Mo. 1945). *Hobson* indicates the very last time a property can be redeemed is when the tax sale purchaser submits their deed application. Back then, issuance and recording of a deed was a ministerial act by the collector, and as discussed elsewhere herein, collectors now have discretion regarding deed issuance. *Wetmore* seems to indicate, less precisely, that recording is the operative moment in time to foreclose redemption. The difference is negligible, but the exact moment in time where the right to redeem is forever barred could make a difference. Imagine a case where a redemptioner tenders after the tax sale purchaser's compliant deed application is fully submitted, but prior to the deed's issuance and/or recording. There has not yet been an appellate case to decide this issue.

CHAPTER 11

GETTING A COLLECTOR'S DEED & THE NATURE OF ITS TITLE

An affidavit to the collector following the requirements of § 140.405 acts as the deed application under § 140.420. The collector uses their discretion to review and either approve or deny the application, along with its attachments, under § 140.405.9(1), but if denied they would normally explain the reasons and give the tax sale purchaser an opportunity to amend or correct any shortcoming or omission.

Once the application is approved, the collector issues and records the deed. The right to redeem is then foreclosed and certain liens are extinguished, assuming proper notice. The collector's deed grantee is vested with an absolute estate in fee simple subject to (1) subsequently due taxes, (2) valid recorded covenants running with the land, (3) easements of record, and (4) easements in use. § 140.420 and § 140.722. Other liens may survive, based on either (a) a statute elevating the lien's priority, or (b) failure of notice to the lien holder.

No title covenants appear on the face of, or otherwise accompany, a collector's deed. A title covenant is essentially a promise by the grantor to the grantee about the nature of the title they are attempting to convey, and how they will assist to defend that title in the future. These are common in private sales but are not present in a tax foreclosure setting. The six title covenants found in a standard general warranty deed are:

Present

(1) seisin [I am the rightful owner];

(2) no encumbrances [there are no undisclosed encumbrances I made];

(3) right to convey [I have the right to sell this property];

Future

(4) quiet enjoyment [you are buying the right to enjoy ownership free of claims of others that they own it];

(5) warranty [I will aid defense if anyone disturbs your quiet enjoyment]; and

(6) further assurance [I will take reasonable steps to assist you in regaining quiet enjoyment of your title, should that be necessary].

A collector's deed has none of these, except perhaps the implicit present covenant of the right to convey. This poses a title insurance problem, even though the deed "creates a new and paramount title to real estate that extinguishes unrecorded leases." *Euclid Plaza Assocs. L.L.C. v. African Am. Law Firm, L.L.C.*, 55 S.W.3d 446 (Mo. App. E.D. 2001).

A tax sale purchaser is the owner of the property on the date the collector's deed is recorded. That is the operative date when the purchaser becomes responsible for charges accruing on the property, such as weeds, condemnation, homeowner's association dues, special assessments, etc., and becomes responsible for casualty and premises liability. The actual date of transfer is relevant often in the case of city code violations and attempted enforcement, some of which efforts take place during the redemption period when the tax sale purchaser has no right to possession and no claim of ownership, having only an inceptive or inchoate property interest.

THE ACTUAL DATE OF TRANSFER IS RELEVANT IN THE CASE OF CITY CODE VIOLATIONS...

CHAPTER 12
POSSESSION & PERSONAL PROPERTY

If entry upon the land is necessary for giving or serving notice, the same is not a trespass. § 140.195.

The purchaser is not entitled to possession of the property during the one-year redemption period. § 140.310 (2015). The old rule was immediate possession for non-homestead properties, which is no longer the law. If unoccupied, the purchaser is entitled to possession after one year. If occupied, an ejectment action is necessary. § 140.580.

Ejectment, not unlawful detainer, is the proper legal path toward possession. Ejectment is under R.S.Mo. § 524.010 *et seq.* and Mo. R. Civ. P. 89. Ejectment claims are regular civil cases, not on a summary track. An ejectment claim may include money damages for rents and profits during the time of wrongful possession. Mo. Approved Jury Instructions 27.03.

For personal property in, upon or at the premises, the tax sale purchaser is confronted with an implied bailment. The purchaser has the same duties as a bailee under such circumstances. " ... where one knowingly comes into possession of a chattel and exercises physical control over it, or where possession has been acquired accidentally, or for some purpose other than bailment, the law imposes on the recipient the duties and obligations of a bailee. 8A Am. Jur. 2d, Bailments Section 38." *Stone v. Crown Diversified Industries Corp.*, 9 S.W.3d 659 (Mo. App. 1999). "Once a bailment relationship, express or implied, is established, it imposes on the bailee a duty to exercise ordinary care in dealing with the bailed property. *Id. citing Lewis v. Lawless Homes, Inc.*, 984 S.W.2d 583, 586 (Mo. App. E.D. 1999).

Ordinary care is a question of fact, and predicting hindsight can be difficult. So err on the side of caution. If a purchaser mistreats or destroys anything, they could have exposure. If belongings are immediately set out on the curb, stolen, destroyed by weather, or put in a dumpster, there could be liability. Consult an attorney with specifics of your situation. Odds are that the attorney will advise the sending of a written notice about the situation and establishment of a reasonable time, place and manner of retrieval.

IF A PURCHASER MISTREATS OR DESTROYS ANYTHING, THEY COULD HAVE EXPOSURE.

For pets or living animals, the answers are less clear but one might consult R.S.Mo. § 340.288 regarding what a veterinarian must do when an animal in their care is abandoned. That might be a reasonable standard of care a court would adopt in such a situation.

CHAPTER 13
QUIETING TITLE

Title to land is not like cash. It is not a tangible, physical object. If it were, possession of the title document is all one would need. Instead, title is intangible and subject to competing claims. Think of it as *noise* about who owns what. An action to quiet title compels these noisy claimants to set forth their claims to be decided by a court. A court quiets the noise, settles any dispute with finality, and perhaps even permanently enjoins the assertion of such claims. Property owners cannot always know who these claimants might be, or what their claims are. So we have title insurance to protect us as necessary. Any buyer would be well-advised to get the most robust policy available, as free as possible from all but standard title policy exceptions.

But back to quiet title actions. A collector's deed grantor (the county collector) stands in the shoes of the former owner. The collector is not the owner themselves. For that reason, most title insurance companies think that has the potential to be quite noisy. In my experience, they're right. Hence a quiet title lawsuit is routine. Quiet title cases require familiarity not just with R.S.Mo. Chapter 140, but also R.S.Mo. Chapter 527. That statute governs declaratory judgment actions. Quiet titles are a species of declaratory judgment.

Most tax sale purchasers, especially sophisticated investors, seek a separate judicial determination of the validity of their deed, as authorized in § 140.330. If they did not take this step, they were left a title that was perhaps marketable, but not typically insurable. *See* Chapter 11. If a purchaser procures a single collector's deed and intends to possess, rent or otherwise utilize the property, without alienating or encumbering it, a quiet title may not be necessary immediately, or at all. There are also some services that purport to issue marketable title when they complete the notice-phase diligence themselves. These self-insured services could work in theory but raise issues beyond the scope of this book.

Quiet title lawsuits are regular civil cases, though sometimes are assigned to associate judges because they seek relief that is under the jurisdictional maximum for such judges. What that means is there is no summary or "bulk" track for these cases. An uncontested case can remain open for generally 90 – 120 days; a contested case may take years to get through the litigation process (discovery, motion practice, trial, post-trial, appeal, etc.).

Ejectment actions may be included. R.S.Mo. § 140.580, *and see* Chapter 12.

The plaintiff in a quiet title case names all parties who have, or may claim to have, an interest in the property. § 140.330.1. Service is accomplished via the regular rules of civil procedure, including where necessary, service by publication for *in rem* suits. Because a collector's deed is a *prima facie* case for plaintiff, a copy is usually attached and incorporated by reference into the allegations of the petition.

A prayer for relief should be carefully crafted to include everything you want the court to do at the outset of the case and at the end of it. It should provide for contingencies such as an invalid sale or deed, reimbursement for improvements and transactional costs, possession issues, and the like. The prayer may have an effect on whether the case is a legal or equitable one, and therefore whether a jury trial may be a right of one of the parties. *See* Chapter 16.

If the tax sale or collector's deed is challenged, a good first step is to retrieve (and at times produce) the entirety of a certified copy of the collector's entire file as well as a certified copy of the collector's deed. Nothing else is required of plaintiff, unless an applicable affirmative defense is properly pleaded with supporting facts and pursued within the rules of civil procedure. Additional discovery may be needed in that case.

The goal of the quiet title is a judicial confirmation of a valid sale and a valid deed transferring an absolute estate in fee simple to plaintiff. This must be done in a way that can make title marketable, so as to clear underwriting at a future closing. If a default judgment is taken on something other than personal service, some title insurance companies may insist on waiting out the one-year period to set aside such a judgment under Mo. R. Civ. P. 74.05(d). An established relationship with a knowledgeable, local title insurance company may be the critical last link in the chain for tax sale purchasers looking to sell property instead of just owning it.

THE QUIET TITLE IS A JUDICIAL CONFIRMATION OF A VALID SALE AND A VALID DEED

Although it seems a tax sale purchaser may be holding all the cards and easily can make a *prima facie* case, courts generally favor redemption and disfavor forfeiture. *Sneil v. Tybe Learning Center, Inc.*, 370 S.W.3d 562, 570 (Mo. banc 2012).

Once a collector's deed grantee obtains a judicial confirmation of the non-judicial foreclosure process, they are more likely to have marketable title (that is, insurable title in a standard real estate closing). But it is not uniform among title companies. Some underwriters refuse the risk categorically. Others impose extensive or insurmountable requirements on the nature of service of process or protracted waiting periods. But knowledgeable and experienced local title insurance companies are more likely to understand and accept such risk, especially after a beneficial relationship has been established over time.

CHAPTER 14

COMMON DEFENSES & AVAILABLE REMEDIES

Any suit by a third party to recover the lands sold for taxes, or otherwise invalidate the collector's deed, must be brought within three years. § 140.590. Challengers often defend but fail to counterclaim for affirmative relief. If a quiet title is successfully defended, a cloud may well remain on the title.

For a challenge to the validity of either the tax sale or the collector's deed to prevail, the injured party must generally plead and prove one of four defense theories, below. If successful, the challenger would be availed of the concomitant remedy, as set forth here:

(1) the sale was inherently defective for one of the limited reasons set forth in R.S.Mo. §§ 140.500 through 140.640 (specifically the three reasons set forth in § 140.530); if proven, the deed is invalid and does not convey good title, and the purchaser would be refunded the taxes paid plus interest from the collector, who may need to be made a party;

(2) the tax sale purchaser failed to comply with the black-letter notice requirements and application for deed as set forth in R.S.Mo. § 140.405 et seq.; if proven, the tax sale purchaser loses any ownership interest and is relegated to a lien for the taxes paid plus interest, pursuant to R.S.Mo. § 140.405.8, citing §§ 140.550 and 140.570 (2015);

(3) notice of the right to redeem fails a constitutional due process standard, as the Missouri tax sale process is, no doubt, a taking of private property by state action; if proven, the deed passes title subject to the unextinguished interest of the lienholder or owner whose constitutional due process rights were violated. *See, e.g., M & P Enterprises, Inc.*, 944 S.W.2d; and/or

(4) some aspect of the sale was contaminated by fraud; needs to be pleaded with factual particularity, and if proven the Missouri courts have indicated in *dicta* that the same might be sufficient in setting aside the deed and/or fashioning some other equitable remedy.

Even somewhat substantial irregularities in the sale process are not sufficient to set aside a sale or invalidate the title passed by a collector's deed, let alone minor grievances and highly technical "gotchas". Chapter 140 is replete with reiterations of this concept:

§ 140.500: A mistake in listing the rightful owner's name does not invalidate a sale.

§ 140.510: Sales have a presumption of validity; any matter not directly affecting the substance of the sale is insufficient to invalidate a sale: no sale is rendered invalid by showing some certificate, return or affidavit was not filed where it is supposed to be.

§ 140.520: no irregularity in any tax sale invalidates a sale or resulting deed, even an omission, an overcharge or failing to perform duties at the time and date specified for performing such duties.

§ 140.620: County records are *prima facie* evidence of the tax sale process.

§ 140.460.2: Collector's deed itself is *prima facie* evidence of the regularity of all proceedings and transfer of valid title.

Two primary provisions govern a suit to set aside a tax deed. First, a challenger to the validity of collector's deed shall set out in their initial petition an offer to refund the purchaser what was paid for the taxes. § 140.600.1. Tender, as it is called, is a mandatory prerequisite of any action against the sale or the deed, though courts have found it non-prejudicial error if the court fashions a similar remedy in its absence. *Glasgow Enterpr., Inc. v. Kusher*, 231 S.W.3d 201 (Mo. App. E.D. 2007) *citing Greenwich Condominium Ass'n. v. Clayton Investment Corp.*, 918 S.W.2d 410, 415 (Mo.App. E.D. 1996).

Second, "[i]n all suits and controversies involving the title of land claimed and held by virtue of the deed executed by the county collector for nonpayment of taxes thereon, under this tax law, the person claiming by adverse title to such deed **shall** be required to prove, in order to defeat the title conveyed by such deed, either that **(1)** the land described therein was not subject to taxation at the date of assessment of the tax for which it was sold, or **(2)** that the taxes for the nonpayment of which the land was sold were paid to the proper officer within the time limited by law therefor [sic], or **(3)** that the same had not been assessed for the taxes for the nonpayment of which it was sold, or **(4)** that the same had been redeemed pursuant to law, or **(5)** that a certificate in proper form had been given by the proper officer, within the time limited by law for paying taxes or for redeeming from sales made for the nonpayment thereof, stating no taxes were due at the time such sale was made, or **(6)** that at the date of the deed the redemption period had not expired." § 140.610 (emphasis and numbering in **bold** added).

Long ago, the Missouri Supreme Court held that common law strict construction of tax sale statutes does not apply. *State ex. Rel Howard v. Timbrook's Estate*, 144 S.W. 843 (1912) (the same legislative power that sets forth the procedures also are used to reduce certain claims to the rank of insufficient technical objections, construing a similar section in a predecessor statute).

In addition to these two statutes, a challenger could also demonstrate disability as previously discussed (R.S.Mo. §§ 140.350 and 140.590). Or a challenger could defend by proving intrinsic or extrinsic fraud. Those claims are rare. More common defenses are failure of statutory notice compliance (§ 140.405) or failure of due process compliance. These defenses are fundamental: they strike right at the core of fair collection of taxes and the enforcement of tax liens.

Tax foreclosures are complex, intricate creatures of statute. No regulations drill down into the fine details of exactly how a sale is conducted. Defendant's attorneys are tempted to claim a particular affidavit was not filed, a particular document was not found where it should be, something immaterial was omitted where it normally would not be, or a particular statement during the sale process was incomplete or inaccurate. These are not valid defenses, but it does not seem to dissuade challengers from trying, whether *pro se* or with the aid of an attorney.

Perhaps the most common defense is a failure to comply with § 140.405, whether in failure to send a notice, failure to send to a certain address, using language that either does not go far enough or goes too far in restating both what is required by statute or due process, or not including everything required in the deed application/affidavit.

Due process defenses regularly attend tax sale challenges as well. *See* Chapter 15.

Different theories of defense avail the challenger of different remedies. Statutory compliance failure can cause a loss of ownership interest and relegate the tax sale purchaser to a lien. Due process failures typically mean the deed is taken subject to the unextinguished interest. Fraud may set aside the entire sale or cause the court to fashion an equitable remedy.

Legal descriptions that fail to identify the parcel with reasonable certainty can invalidate a sale or deed. The description needs to be accurate in four places: (1) the collector's pre-sale published notice, (2) the collector's pre-sale mailed notices, (3) the purchaser's post-sale notices of the right to redeem, and (4) the collector's deed. Certain abbreviations in certain places are allowed. § 140.180.

This does not mean the description must be perfect. Extrinsic evidence is admissible to clarify an error or uncertainty in the legal description. *See* Chapter 8. The description must be reasonably certain, such that it is enough to allow someone reasonably skilled in locating property boundaries to identify the property. *See generally Stadium W. Props., LLC v. Johnson*, 133 S.W.3d 128 (Mo. App. W.D. 2004); *Wayward, Inc. v. Shafer*, 936 S.W.2d 843 (Mo. App. E.D. 1996); *Podlesak v. Wesley*, 849 S.W.2d 728 (Mo. App. S.D. 1993) (sufficiency of legal description is a question of fact for trial).

If the legal description is so flawed that a surveyor cannot decipher it, the three-year statute of limitations to challenge a deed does not apply. *Braun v. Petty*, 31 S.W.3d 521 (Mo. App. E.D. 2000) (collector's deed void on its face for vagueness in description, limitations period does not apply).

IF THE LEGAL DESCRIPTION IS INDECIPHERABLE... THE STATUTE OF LIMITATIONS DOES NOT APPLY.

Adequacy of consideration was and is not a factor in determining the validity of the administrative procedures in Chapter 140, at least in third offerings. *Powell v. County of St. Louis*, 559 S.W.2d 189 (Mo. banc 1977). It may remain a question as to whether this holding applies to a first or second offering sale, but it does not appear anyone has seriously tried since 1977. The defense is referred to as constructive fraud, but likely would not set aside a tax sale merely because the taxes due were less than the supposed fair market value of the property, but instead would be considered in the context of a forced sale to protect the state's fundamental interest in revenue. *Id.*

Standing may be a valid strategy in upholding the validity of a collector's deed, if the challenger fails to set up their own title with evidence. *Scott v. Unknown Heirs of Solomon Garrison*, 235 S.W.2d 372 (Mo. 1951).

Another valid strategy in upholding a tax sale is ratification by the challenger, if that same challenger has claimed and procured the sale surplus. Ratification may estop said challenger from both enjoying the benefits of the sale and yet challenging its validity nevertheless. *See discussion in WMAC 2013, LLC v. Noreen Moore, et al.,* Case No. 15SL-CC00900, trial judgment for tax sale purchaser, *citing Lytle v. Page,* 591 S.W.2d 421, 424 (Mo. App. S.D. 1979) ("There is no rule of equity more firmly settled and more just and reasonable than that one who knowingly receives the purchase price of his own estate sold by one assuming to act under a valid power estops himself, in equity, from denying the power," *citing cases); Proctor v. Nance,* 119 S.W. 409, 411 (Mo. 1909).

CHAPTER 15

CONSTITUTIONAL DUE PROCESS, PRE- & POST-SALE

PRE-SALE NOTICES

R.S.Mo. § 140.150.2 requires the collector to send notice to the <u>owner</u> by regular mail prior to publishing notice under R.S.Mo. § 140.170. If the assessed value of the property exceeds $1,000, a certified mail notice to the <u>owner</u> is required before publishing as well. Similar to post-sale notices, and in accordance with *Jones v. Flowers*, if the certified mail notice is returned unsigned, the collector must resend this second notice by regular mail to the <u>owner</u> and to "occupant." The lack of actual receipt changes nothing about the tax liability.

Tax sales are a taking of private property interests by state action. One previous case indicated the property interests of owners and lien holders are affected before the taking is complete by way of a collector's deed. *Investment Corp. of the Virginias, Inc. v. Acquaviva*, 302 S.W.3d 195, 199 (Mo. App. E.D. 2009) *citing inter alia Schwartz v. Dey*, 665 S.W.2d 933

(Mo. banc 1984) (stating pre-sale mailed notice is required if addresses are available or reasonably ascertainable, and if returned, additional steps are required "*if it is practicable to do so*"). In reality, it seems it is never practicable for the collector to do more than they already do. But evidence may need to be adduced on the issue to demonstrate the point. *See* trial record in *FWR Holdings, LLC v. Regions Bank, et al.*, Clay County Case No. 10CY-CV12540 (2012).

The Eastern District recently refused to find, categorically, that due process requires pre-sale mailed notice to lien holders. *JD Wealth LLC v. U.S. Bank National Association ND, et al.*, ED111572 (12/19/23) (regional reporter citation not yet available). *JD Wealth* makes it clear each case will be judged on its own facts; there is no bright-line rule to be followed.

POST-SALE NOTICES

"Lack of receipt does not prove lack of due process." *JD Wealth LLC v. U.S. Bank National Association ND, et al.*, ED111572 at p. 23 (12/19/23) (regional reporter citation not yet available). Properly viewed, lack of receipt is the beginning, not the end, of the legal analysis. The challenger must demonstrate what procedures for notice were utilized and what aspect(s) of the same were insufficient. *JD Wealth LLC v. U.S. Bank National Association ND, et al.*, ED111572 at 23 (12/19/23) (regional reporter citation not yet available).

Failure to comply with applicable statutes entails the remedy provided therein. Failure to comply with due process results in the owner or lienholder's interest surviving, and the collector's deed is taken subject thereto. *See, e.g., Anheuser-Busch Empl. Credit Union v. Davis*, 899 S.W.2d 868 (Mo. banc 1995) (third sale where no written notice ever was sent to mortgagee unconstitutional, deed taken subject to the mortgage). A court applies both of these parallel concepts if properly challenged: statutory and due process compliance. In this context, due process is <u>notice and an opportunity to be heard prior to a pending taking of a private property interest by state action</u>. That oversimplifies it a bit but is an apt working definition.

Prior to 1983, the only notice of a tax sale, pre- or post-sale, was by publication. The primary case in point was *Mullane v. Centr. Hanover Bank & Tr. Co.*, 339 U.S. 306 (1950). That case limited the analysis of constitutional due process to what the sender knew *ex ante*, that is, at the time notice was sent. There was no discussion of what the sender learned *post hoc*, or after the fact.

In 1983 both the United States Supreme Court and the Missouri Supreme Court issued opinions saying it was not constitutionally sufficient to ignore what the sender later learned about their attempts at notice, where a taking of private property rights by state action occurs. *Mennonite Bd. of Missions v. Adams*, 462 U.S 791 (1983); *Lohr v. Cobur Corp.*, 654 S.W.2d 883 (Mo. banc 1983). Shortly thereafter, § 140.405 was amended and began to take on its modern form. It provided for a post-sale notice sent by the tax sale purchaser, rather than the state. Though the country's ideas of due process were evolving, collectors took on no additional time or expense in meeting this new standard. The state simply delegated the responsibility to tax sale purchasers. It is the tax sale

IT IS THE TAX SALE PURCHASER, NOT THE STATE, AT WHOSE LONE PERIL NOTICES MUST BE PROPER AND TIMELY.

purchaser, not the State, at whose lone peril notices must be proper and timely.

The case law developed further, demonstrating how § 140.405 really was a product of an evolving understanding of due process. Statutory compliance alone was not always enough, to the great confusion of the novice tax sale purchaser. In *Jones v. Flowers*, 547 U.S. 220 (2006), the U.S. Supreme Court held that a certified mail notice of an Arkansas tax sale returned "unclaimed" triggered the state's obligation to undertake further notice efforts, such as sending by regular mail, posting, or addressing otherwise undeliverable mail to "occupant". *Jones* reiterated some of the same themes as *Mullane* but added a *post hoc* analysis – now it mattered what the sender learned about their attempted notice after its dispatch. A few years later, the Missouri Supreme Court followed suit in *Schlereth v. Hardy*, 280 S.W.3d 47 (Mo. banc 2009), parroting the language of *Jones* (state must make further efforts if certified mail is returned unclaimed, "if it is practicable to do so.").

The *Schlereth* court indicated use of a process server may be a reasonable further measure. *Id.* at 52. Practitioners received even better guidance from a Chapter 141 case in *Foreclosure of Liens for Delinquent Land Taxes v. Holton*, 428 S.W.3d 670 (Mo. App. W.D. 2014). There the county made three unsuccessful attempts by certified mail, one unsuccessful attempt by regular mail, and one unsuccessful attempt to post notice (it was a condo with restricted access), in addition to publishing prior to the Chapter 141 sale. The court found the government could have done more, by at least doing the things suggested in *Jones*: sending regular mail (which they did), posting a notice on the property (which they tried but could not), and addressing mail to "occupant" (which they did not do). It was this third prong they failed, and because it was relatively easy to do, and the property was not vacant land, due process required it.

The *Holton* Court also discussed allegations that the tax sale purchaser could have done a simple Google search, but the court rejected this argument, saying the government is not required to do open-ended searches for new addresses. Then the court delved into the property owner's comparative fault in failing their duty to preserve their property. This case is a must read to understand the fact-intensiveness as to what due process requires.

The *JD Wealth* Court reiterated the holdings in *Holton*, stating "... additional steps are needed only when the evidence shows the government had knowledge that notice to the owner was not received." *JD Wealth LLC v. U.S. Bank National Association ND, et al.*, ED111572 at 27 (12/19/23) (regional reporter citation not yet available) *citing In re Foreclosures of Liens for Delinquent Land Taxes by Action in rem Collector of Revenue v. Bhatti*, 334 S.W.3d 444, 451 (Mo. banc 2011) (the court "cannot impose new requirements when there has been no constitutional violation."). It is the challenger's burden to prove the constitutional violation. *JD Wealth* at 22, *citing Usery v. Turner Elkhorn Mining Co.*, 428 U.S. 1 (1976).

Immediately after *JD Wealth*, another tax sale case was decided by the Eastern District Court of Appeals. *In re Foreclosures of Liens for Delinquent Land Taxes by Action in rem, Collector of Revenue v. Reibe, et al.*, ED111425 (1/23/24) (regional reporter citation not yet available). In *Reibe*, the City of St. Louis judicially foreclosed a property under R.S.Mo. Chapter 92. The Court set aside the sale prior to its confirmation, finding insufficient notice. The Eastern District Court of Appeals reversed and upheld the sale. A beneficiary deed from the deceased owner was recorded, but no death recital was recorded so the beneficiary deed grantee (the owner's sole heir) did not show in the assessor's records as the titled owner. The court found statutory compliance that included mailings, posting at the courthouse, publication, and posting at the property. Again the court weighed the tax sale challenger's inaction in preserving his property interests, listing out due diligence acts the challenger could have, or perhaps should have, done to alert authorities of his ownership. *Citing Holton*, at p. 4 and p. 6 of the opinion.

The presumption is that these cases are instructive, even though they talk in terms of a state actor. Whereas a tax sale purchaser is not a state actor, they certainly stand in the shoes of the state for purposes of sending notice compliant with due process. Whether the analysis changes for a private actor standing in the shoes of the State is unknown with certainty at this time. For other helpful due process cases, see *Crossland v. Thompson*, 317 S.W.3d 635 (Mo. App. S.D. 2010), and *Prescott v. Mo. Dept. of Soc. Servs.*, WD77389 (Mo. App. W.D. 2015) (and cited cases within each).

Additional efforts a purchaser could take perhaps include public record searches, skip traces, publication, sending electronic mail, sending notice via a private messaging function on a social media site, or texting a cell phone number known to belong to the intended recipient. To date, both Missouri and federal courts have stopped short of requiring these particular measures, and neither requires open-ended name or address searches of public records or the internet.

A cautious purchaser might go beyond what is required in a particularly important matter. The idea is to make noticing efforts consistent with someone who had a real desire to achieve actual notice. At least one trial court ruled for the tax sale purchaser where the challenger argued for a method of notice that would not have achieved actual notice even if undertaken. *Harpagon MO, LLC v. James Howard, et al.*, Clay County Case No. 08CY-CV03032 (2008) (IRS argued notice should have been sent to an address that was admittedly defunct, court held the law does not require a futile act, judgment for tax sale purchaser, appeal dismissed).

There are other applicable due process cases, this is not nearly exhaustive. For our summary purposes here, suffice it to say a tax sale purchaser is on notice that strict statutory compliance may not be enough, and the question of whether their efforts undertaken toward notice were sufficient is a fact question, decided on a case-by-case basis under the totality of circumstances, both *ex ante* and *post hoc.*

Best practice suggests doing as much as reasonably practicable under all circumstances. The courts seem to be steering us back to a very fact-specific analysis, with a hyper-focus on *Jones.* Preparing all fact testimony and evidence necessary to demonstrate compliance after the fact is wise, but of course must be weighed against the attendant costs of time, effort, expense and opportunity cost.

If some specific further step or effort is impracticable, it is not required. But that is largely a question of evidence, and then the opinion of the fact finder. Practicability is subjective, or if objective at least not clearly defined.

A collector's testimony about time limitations, staff limitations, exorbitant costs, or the like, may be needed. If done well, that type of testimony – that the collector could not have practicably done anything more – could be enough for a court to reject a defendant's argument that more was required. In fact, *Acquaviva* (regarding pre-sale notices) was remanded for precisely that reason – to develop a record as to what was, or was not, practicable for the collector to do. For an example of this type of testimony that was successful in the face of such a defense, see the trial judgment for the tax sale purchaser in *FWR Holdings, LLC v. Regions Bank, et al.*, Clay County Case No. 10CY-CV12540 (2012).

NOTICE LANGUAGE

The above discussion revolves around further efforts in cases of "non-received" notices. When the notice actually reaches its intended recipient, does it nevertheless do enough to comply with due process? When a recipient gets a notice, what content or language must it include to discharge the notice obligation imposed by the U.S. Constitution? Turning now to those questions, it is not as simple as one might think.

Merely following the statute as to post-sale notices of the right to redeem, one might miss the constitutional requirement to communicate *pendency* of an action against the recipient in their notice of the right to redeem. The statute mandates only indicating the *existence* of a right. To communicate *pendency*, as opposed to mere *existence*, is a constitutional case law concept not found in Chapter 140. Yet due process clearly has something to say about the *content* of the notice of the right to redeem.

The general rule is that "parties whose rights would be affected by a tax sale be afforded notice reasonably calculated under all of the circumstances to apprise them of the pendency of the action." *Mennonite Bd. of Missions v. Adams*, 462 U.S. 791 (1983).

The touchstone is notification that "the matter is pending," not that "some particular step must be taken or that certain procedure be followed ..." *Mullane v. Cent. Hanover*

Bank & Trust Co., 339 U.S. 306, 314 (1950). The recipient of a
due process notice is not entitled to precise legal advice about
what they might or should do. *See e.g. State v. Goodbar*, 297
S.W.2d 525, 528 (Mo. 1957); *accord Atkins v. Parker*, 472 U.S.
115 (1985) ("The entire structure of our democratic government rests on the premise that the individual citizen is ca-
pable of informing himself about the particular policies that
affect his destiny."); *quoted in City of West Covina v. Perkins*,
525 U.S. 234 (1999). A recipient "must be held to a knowledge
of the law." *Bishop v. Bd. of Educ. of Francis Howell Sch. Dist.*,
575 S.W.2d 827, 829 (Mo. App. E.D. 1978).

Therefore *United Asset Mgmt. Trust Co. v. Clark*, 332
S.W.3d 159 (Mo. App. W.D. November 30, 2010) held, "…
there is no due process requirement to inform those receiv-
ing notice of the specific time limits applicable for redemption, the specific procedures that must be followed, or any
other specific details, nor is there any such requirement in §
140.405." *United Asset*, 332 S.W.3d at 175. *See also City of West
Covina v. Perkins*, 525 U.S. 234, 240 (1999).

In *United Asset*, the Missouri Court of Appeals for the
Western District stated, "[t]he fact that the notice stated that
[Trust] had ninety days in which to redeem the property is of
no consequence," at least in part because the Clarks' collector's deed was recorded *exactly* ninety days after the date of
the letter and therefore was not misleading. 332 S.W.3d at 175.

The Eastern District issued an opinion on this subject
about a year after the Western District's *United Asset* opinion.
Ndegwa v. KSSO, LLC, No. ED96315, 2011 WL 4790633 (Mo.
App. E.D. Oct. 11, 2011)[4]. The *Ndegwa* Court disagreed and

---

4   Note that Ndegwa was transferred to the Missouri Supreme Court and was
     decided 7/3/12 along with Harpagon and Sneil. Ndegwa v. KSSO, LLC, 371 S.W.3d
     798 (Mo. banc). In that part of the case, which functions as an original appeal

distinguished *United Asset's* due process cases. The *Ndegwa* notice stated, in relevant part:

> ... the Missouri Status [sic] afford you the opportunity to redeem and/or otherwise protect your interest. Be further advised, that this opportunity will be available for a period of not less than 90 days from the date of this letter ... it is possible that the period of redemption may exceed the 90 day period described in this notice. This indication ... is not brought to your attention as an inducement for you to expect an extended period ... If you fail to redeem this property within the redemption period, you will be forever barred from redeeming the property. *Ndegwa*, 2011 WL 4790633 at 2.

This notice was found to be insufficient for failure to use "one year" language regarding the redemption period. *Ndegwa* also drew a distinction between notifying the recipient of the "pendency" of an action versus the "existence" of an action, holding a tax sale notice must include a time component. 2011 WL 4790633 at 8. Recall *United Asset* does not require statement of any time component to comply with the statute or due process. *Accord Harpagon MO, LLC v. Clay County Collector*, 2011 WL 864926 (Mo. App. W.D. #72006, 2011).

Ndegwa comes to a conclusion that can be broken down into two separate and distinct subparts: (1) a notice "must

---

under Missouri law, the Missouri Supreme Court dismissed the appeal for lack of finality in the judgment of the trial court. In other words, it was dismissed on procedural grounds. However, the Missouri Supreme Court went on to decide most of the relevant issues in the companion case, Sneil, LLC v. Tybe Learning Center, Inc., 370 S.W.3d 562 (Mo. banc 7/3/12).

include a time component to comport with due process"; and (2) the time component to be included is provided by Missouri statute – one year.

Ndegwa Subpart Two deals with *when* a notice must be sent. To the extent that holding ever was correct, it is no longer after the legislature amended the statutes in 2013 to redefine when the purchaser is authorized to acquire the deed in R.S.Mo. § 140.405.9. *Boston* and *United Asset* may once again correctly state the law as it currently sits, but that is untested in the courts of appeal at the time of this writing.

Ndegwa Subpart One dealt with *what time component, if any* must be stated in the notice. This is a critical distinction because the due process cases support the conclusion drawn by *Ndegwa* Subpart One, even though the *Ndegwa* court veered in the wrong direction in Subpart Two. The cases cited by *United Asset* use a derivative of the word "pendency" as opposed to "existence," and that distinction is important in a due process analysis. *See Mennonite*, 462 U.S. 791 (uses the word "pendency"); *Ndegwa* at 9 ("the seriousness, scope and permanency of the taking" are all greater in tax sale cases). *Ndegwa* holds, in part, that a notice "must include a time component to comport with due process" and the same can be accomplished without being so precise or specific that it constitutes legal advice. 2011 WL 4790633 at 8. *Ndegwa's* insight is of possible value in this regard.

In *Sneil v. Tybe Learning Center, Inc.*, the Missouri Supreme Court at least partially weighed in on these issues. 370 S.W.3d 562 (Mo. banc 2012). Note, this case was decided the same day as the dismissal of *Ndegwa*[5] and the opinion in

---

[5]   The Ndegwa case discussed here is that which took place at the Missouri Supreme Court stage; the citations to Ndegwa above are from the appeal in the Eastern District which preceded transfer.

Harpagon. The shortcoming of this case, insofar as its contribution to this discussion, is twofold: (1) the *Sneil* notice stated no duration of the redemption period, and (2) the court held the notice was not timely for the same reason as *Harpagon*, and as discussed elsewhere in this book, those holdings were legislatively abrogated. But let us discuss *Sneil*, because there the Missouri Supreme Court analyzed not just timeliness of the notice but also its content.

Helpfully, *Sneil* acknowledges the flawed premise of putting too much weight on older tax sale cases under previous versions of the statute, which ironically now applies reflexively to *Sneil* itself due to the aforementioned legislative abrogation. 370 S.W.3d at 571 (discussing how appellant's reliance on a 1942 tax sale opinion was misplaced in light of the fact it was a third offering as opposed to first/second, but also because "the relevant statutes have been amended multiple times since ..."); *A.L. 2015 H.B. 613.*

The *Sneil* court agreed that nothing in the text of § 140.405 requires telling the recipient when the deadline to redeem is. The court cautions against electing to include an amount of time the recipient has to redeem, and indicates that if a purchaser so elects, he or she "must indicate the correct amount of time." *Sneil,* 370 S.W.3d at 572.

And then, in what strikes me as *dicta*, the Supreme Court states, "Due process does not require that the notice include the time frame in which the owner must exercise the right to redeem." *Id.* Alternatively, the court stated, recipients are held to a knowledge of the law, and it is not the tax sale purchaser's obligation to inform them of available remedial measures. *Id.*

Lastly, the *Sneil* Court held "a purchaser does not need to indicate that the recipient has one year from the date of the tax sale to redeem the property to comply with due process."

Id. at 572-3 (reversing prior Eastern District cases such as *Ce-darBridge*, 293 S.W.3d at 465).

Sneil perhaps liberates purchasers from the stricter formulations of previous Eastern District cases, and definitively holds that the 90-day time period is sufficient as a matter of law. 370 S.W.3d at 572-3, fn. 10. But again, recall that the primary basis of the holding in *Sneil* is the interpretation of the "authorized to acquire a deed" language and finding the notice untimely. That construction of the language was legislatively abrogated shortly thereafter, as the legislature went back and explicitly defined "authorized to acquire a deed" within § 140.405. So, how much of *Sneil* is still good law? We do not know for sure until an appellate court revisits the issue.

Therefore, as to *what time component, if any,* must be stated in Missouri tax sale notices of the right to redeem perhaps can be summarized as follows:

1. To comply with Missouri statute, the inclusion of a time component is not required. *United Asset*, 332 S.W.3d 159.

2. To comply with due process, a general time component that is not so specific or precise so as to constitute legal advice but sufficiently communicates *pendency*, should be stated. *Ndegwa*, 2011 WL 4790633.

3. The time component to be stated may depend on *when* the notice is sent:

   a. if sent prior to ninety days before the automatic one-year period of redemption, one year language may be sufficient to communicate pendency; or

b. if sent anytime after ninety days before the automatic one-year period of redemption, ninety-day language may be sufficient to communicate pendency; but

c. regardless of the date of dispatch, it may be sufficient either to quote the statutory language or include a copy of the relevant statutes (the latter option of which is suggested by the *Sneil* court in fn. 10).

No court has confirmed this as applicable Missouri law. The current state of the law is unsettled. This explanation seems to comport with both Jones-Munger and due process but is yet to pass judicial scrutiny. However, this approach is at odds with some of the case law interpreting prior versions of the statute. *See, e.g., Keylien Corp. v. Johnson*, 284 S.W.3d 606, 613 (Mo. App. E.D. 2009); *Drake Dev. & Constr., LLC v. Jacob Holdings, Inc.*, 306 S.W.3d 171, 174 (Mo. App. S.D. 2010). While this approach is untested, it is at least equally dangerous to say in conclusory fashion only that a right to redeem exists.

Though not required by the plain language of Missouri statutes, to comply with due process, the notice language must communicate a sense of *urgency*. The due process cases talk about pendency of an adverse action, not mere existence of a right. Without that sense of urgency conveyed, a tax sale purchaser perhaps violates a recipient's due process rights, whether they actually receive and read the notice or not. Until clarified, every

...THE NOTICE LANGUAGE MUST COMMUNICATE A SENSE OF URGENCY.

dispatcher of tax sale notices does their best to comply and hopes for the best.

Under a due process analysis, *ex ante* the best information a tax sale purchaser can give is a generally applicable time frame that communicates pendency, without being so specific in detail so as to rise to the level of giving legal advice. The definition of "authorized to acquire the deed" included in the 2013 amendment to § 140.405.9 abrogates the timeliness holdings in *Bosch* and *Sneil*. Because the precise date of recording the collector's deed is impossible to project, it may be unwise to get too specific.

Tax sales have been invalidated where courts have found the notices inaccurate or misleading. *Hames v. Bellistri*, 300 S.W.3d 235, 239 (Mo. E.D. 2009). All a tax sale purchaser knows is they intend the collector's deed recording date to be after the one year, and before the certificate expires in eighteen months. The precise date of recording depends on numerous unpredictable factors. These are outside the purchaser's knowledge, and guessing is ill-advised.

CHAPTER 16
JURY TRIALS?

Even most attorneys have a difficult time telling which claims are entitled to a jury trial in Missouri and which are not. "The problem of determining whether a jury trial should occur in cases involving claims for both damages and equitable relief is not new, nor is it simple, in Missouri or elsewhere. See generally, Right in Equity Suit to Jury Trial of Counterclaim Involving Legal Issue, 17 A.L.R.3d 1321 (William E. Shipley et al. eds., 1968) (overview of how different states have resolved this issue). This Court has addressed the issue, directly and indirectly, on numerous occasions. In its present state, the law in Missouri is inconsistent and confusing." *State ex rel. Leonardi v. Sherry*, 137 S.W.3d 462, 465 (Mo. 2004).

The *Leonardi* Court describes how once a court of equity acquires jurisdiction, and then it becomes apparent monetary relief will be necessary, generally the court will retain jurisdiction and afford complete relief by assessing legal damages (money), which is normally the province of a jury. *Id.* "Another line of cases, however, states that 'a court of equity does not have jurisdiction to render a judgment for a plaintiff on legal issues in the absence of a finding that some equitable right of the plaintiff has also been violated,' *Krummenacher v. Western Auto Supply Co.*, 217 S.W.2d 473, 475 (1949), and 'where a case for relief in equity fails, a court of equity is without jurisdiction to award other relief by way of disposing of the entire controversy; unless, indeed, it appears that the remedy at law will be inadequate.' *Jaycox v. Brune*, 434 S.W.2d 539, 543 (Mo. 1968)." *Id.* at 466.

Equitable relief is coercive relief such as specific performance, declaratory judgment, injunctions, some types of restitution, reformation of a deed, abatement of a nuisance, and the like. Legal relief is monetary damages, which is reserved as a role for juries. However, even upon equitable claims, a trial judge may award money damages as part of the relief for violations of equitable rights. *State ex rel. Willman v. Sloan*, 574 S.W.2d 421 (Mo. banc 1978). And of course, though the right to jury remains inviolate consistent with the Missouri constitution, a party is free to waive such right in any given case.

The *Leonardi* Court sought to clarify the morass we borrowed from old England in this regard, noting the "historical preference for trial by jury expressed in Article I, section 22(a) of the Constitution of the State of Missouri." 137 S.W.3d at 468 (overuse of "equitable cleanup" doctrine to prevent jury trials on legal claims is inconsistent with preference for jury trials). *Leonardi* held that trials should be conducted to allow the legal claims to be tried to a jury, with the court reserving for its own determination only equitable claims and defenses, which it should decide consistently with the factual findings made by the jury. *Paraphrased in State ex rel. Barker v. Tobben*, 311 S.W.3d 798 (Mo. 2010). Trial courts in Missouri ever since have had to use discretion in determining what claims get a jury and which do not. Incidental claims at law being tried to the court (equitable cleanup) should be the exception, not the rule. *Id.*

Missouri courts have "held that a quiet title judgment is a <u>legal</u> remedy when the petition does not seek to set aside any deed or instrument and the relief granted is 'only a determination of the existing title as between litigants.'" *Massachusetts General Life Ins. Co. v. Sellers*, 835 S.W.2d 475, 483 (Mo. App. S.D. 1992) (<u>underline</u> added for emphasis); *see also Erwin v. City of Palmyra*, 119 S.W.3d 582, 586-86 (Mo. App. E.D. 2003) (a quiet title action is an action at law when there is no request for affirmative equitable relief and the issue is a determination of the existing title as between litigants); *as cited in State ex rel. Barker v. Tobben*, 311 S.W.3d 798 (Mo. 2010).

Most tax sale quiet titles are likely legal claims under the above descriptions, as most seek only a declaration as to the relative title claims of the parties to the suit. Thus, such actions are subject to jury trial at the election of any litigant, whether it be the tax sale purchaser, former owner, lien holder, collector, or otherwise. Some such quiet title suits seek various forms of statutory protections if the deed is to be set aside, some of which might amount to equitable relief. Assuming for the moment said requests for contingent relief do not convert the otherwise legal claims, a typical tax sale quiet title gives the litigants the choice of whether they want a bench trial, by waiving the right to jury trial, or a jury trial by simply invoking the state constitutional right to the same. A bench trial would occur only if all parties agree to waive the right to jury trial.

It is common for a tax sale quiet title case to be combined with an action for ejectment, as possession of the property can be at stake. Unlawful detainer actions, which are summary proceedings with specific procedural rules, are generally not available to a tax sale purchaser to obtain possession. Therefore, in order to save time and costs, an ejectment action within the quiet title case makes sense – both are civil actions and both may be necessary to provide complete relief. Ejectment claims include monetary damages for rents and profits or other use of the land during the time of wrongful possession, plus an order allowing a writ of possession to be issued. Ejectment actions are legal, not equitable, claims, and thus also are subject to a jury. Mo. Approved Jury Instructions 27.03. *See* Chapter 12.

TO SAVE TIME AND COSTS, AN EJECTMENT ACTION WITHIN THE QUIET TITLE CASE MAKES SENSE

Another question is what if a standard tax sale quiet title is met with affirmative defenses and/or a counterclaim primarily seeking equitable relief for which a jury is not available? Most challengers to a tax sale or collector's deed seek some form of setting aside the deed, which is purely equitable. That portion, when alleged, would attach equitable jurisdiction and prevent the challenger from seeking a jury on it. In most cases, a bench trial makes the litigation faster and cheaper, which is probably in the best interest of the tax sale purchaser.

The question is, at the point an equitable counterclaim is made, whether a tax sale purchaser could seek a jury trial on its claims yet keep the challenger's equitable claims severed and reserved for the judge, to be decided consistent with the jury's findings of fact. If the challenger would rather have their claims to set aside a collector's deed decided by a jury, the question is the inverse of equitable cleanup.

In equitable cleanup, a judge proceeds with awarding legal relief (money) in an otherwise equity case. What we broach here is the inverse – legal cleanup – where a challenger to a collector's deed would seek to have its equitable claims decided by a jury. That seems unlikely: there is no such doctrine as "legal cleanup."

This dynamic also begs the question: if a challenger wants a jury trial, would they be best off *not* raising affirmative defenses or counterclaims seeking equitable relief? If the challenger gets to a jury and wins, but has not filed a counterclaim, is there not still a cloud remaining on the title at the conclusion of the case? Would the court then fashion the equitable relief necessary under the statute? These are questions without obviously available answers.

To determine what is a legal or equitable claim, the relief sought is key. When a tax sale purchaser asks only for a declaration, it is likely a legal claim for which a jury can be had. By contrast, a former homeowner's counterclaim to set aside such a deed is equitable in nature and cannot be tried to a jury. Such equitable claims are not converted to legal claims by a prayer for costs or fees. "The fact that [a party's] prayer for relief requested costs and fees incurred in bringing the action and included a general prayer for 'such other and further relief' deemed just and proper' did not convert [the party's] equitable action into one at law subject to a demand for jury trial. *Cf. Fischer v. First Am. Title Ins. Co.*, 388 S.W.3d 181, 185 n.2 (Mo. App. W.D. 2012) (the prayer for relief in a lawsuit is not a separate cause of action)." *Deutsche Bank Nat'l Trust Co. v. Pyle*, 518 S.W.3d 805, 817-818 (Mo. App. 2017).

There is no clear case law in the context of a Missouri tax sale quiet title action yet. Ultimately, and consistent with the holding of *Leonardi*, the judge in a tax sale quiet title likely has discretion to submit the legal claims to the jury – on the purchaser's case-in-chief and upon ejectment. The judge would reserve for the court's separate determination the equitable questions – on setting aside the deed. The court would, in theory, award equitable relief, or deny the same, consistent with the jury's findings of fact, and provide the required statutory remedies to the purchaser if the challenger prevails.

CHAPTER 17

EFFECT OF A BANKRUPTCY FILING

Some tax distressed owners seek protection from administrative tax foreclosure by filing a Chapter 13 bankruptcy. Most bankruptcy filings trigger the automatic stay – a pause on collection activity as to pre-petition debts. At least some bankruptcy filers, and their attorneys, think they can pay the taxes off over the bankruptcy plan, which can last three to five years.

In the Eighth Circuit, the federal territory that includes Missouri, expiration of redemption periods for real property taxes under state law are not affected by the automatic stay and cannot be tolled by the filing of a bankruptcy, subject to an additional sixty (60) days granted by 11 U.S.C. § 108(b). *In re Froehle*, 286 B.R. 94, 98 (8th Cir. BAP 2002); *accord In re Boykin*, 437 B.R. 346 (Bankr. E.D. Mo. 2010).

The collector cannot enforce Chapter 140 against a property that is in receivership or in bankruptcy without leave of the court having jurisdiction over it. *Davison v. Arne*, 248 S.W.2d 582 (Mo. Supp. 1952). A collector may face a suit for damages for an improper sale in this context, which could include actual damages and a ten percent penalty upon the collector's bond, under §§ 140.300.2 or 140.490. So, a county collector will tread lightly around a receivership or bankruptcy.

Generally current taxes have a priority unsecured status and may be reimbursed by a bankruptcy trustee, but delinquent back-taxes are mere unsecured debt. A bankruptcy can wipe out an *in personam* obligation of the debtor to pay taxes, but only if the debtor successfully obtains a discharge. And remember, Chapter 140 is all about making the land pay for the taxes, not the person.

All of which is to say, the *in personam* obligation may be discharged, but the *in rem* obligation may remain. To avoid a lien, a separate adversary proceeding must be undertaken within the bankruptcy case.

So, Chapter 140 still has enforcement potential even when the owner files for bankruptcy protection. However, leave of court in the form of relief from the automatic stay, or perhaps a motion confirming the stay does not apply to non-estate property, is a practical necessity. With a well-written brief in the bankruptcy court, this obstacle has been, and

CHAPTER 140 STILL HAS ENFORCEMENT POTENTIAL EVEN WHEN THE OWNER FILES FOR BANKRUPTCY PROTECTION.

likely can be, overcome. *See, e.g., In re: Anne Lucille Barton*, Bankruptcy Case No. 19-42134-drd13 (Bkr. Mo. W.D. 2019), Doc. 24, 26, and 47; *In re: Angela K. Ryan*, Bankruptcy Case No. 14-42903-abf13 (Bkr. Mo. W.D. 2014), Doc. 25 and 33.

There are also other situations where an automatic stay does not apply in bankruptcy, such as multiple new bankruptcy filings in a short period of time. *See, e.g., In Re:*

Jamison Avion Stiriling, Case No. 16-47912 (Mo. E.D. Bkr.) Doc. No. 10 (Order on Motion for Order Confirming Automatic Stay is Inapplicable, stating "11 U.S.C. § 362(c)(3)(A) applies and the stay provided by 11 U.S.C. § 362(a) was terminated with respect to the debtor 30 days after" the bankruptcy filing date, where the individual debtor had a previous pending case dismissed in the preceding one year).

With leave of court in hand, the collector would typically feel comfortable enough to then issue the deed regardless of the pending bankruptcy. If the deed already was issued during the pending bankruptcy, a prudent investor likely would want relief from the stay prior to filing a quiet title action. A timely objection to the Chapter 13 plan may help accomplish this goal.

CHAPTER 18

INVALID SALES OR COLLECTOR'S DEEDS

Protection of the tax sale purchaser's investment is a central theme of Jones-Munger. A challenger must plead tender under § 140.600, which is another way of saying the challenger must offer to refund the taxes and interest due the tax sale purchaser. An owner does not get a windfall of having their taxes paid gratuitously, in the event they are able to prevail in setting aside the sale or deed. But failure to plead tender was not fatal, where the trial court fashioned the same remedy and satisfied the intent of the statute where the challenger did not. *Glasgow Enterpr., Inc. v. Kusher*, 231 S.W.3d 201 (Mo. App. E.D. 2007) *citing Greenwich Condominium Assoc. v. Clayton Investment Corp.*, 918 S.W.2d 410, 415 (Mo. App. E.D. 1996).

If a deed is to be found invalid, the quiet title is not dismissed, but the court instead ascertains the amount of taxes paid (both principally and in subsequently due taxes) and orders it paid within a reasonable time, plus up to 10% interest. § 140.330.2. If unpaid thereafter, the court orders that the interest is sold, and the equity of redemption is forever foreclosed. That sale proceeds in this priority: sale of rents and profits for seven years, then the property interest of the person ordered to pay, then a life estate of the person ordered to pay, and lastly the fee simple of such land, whichever is necessary to bring in a sufficient amount to pay back the tax sale purchaser. § 140.330.3 and 330.4.

Under most circumstances, an invalid deed does not cause loss of all interest in the property. Instead, a lien in favor of the tax sale purchaser is provided by statute. § 140.550 and 570. This has come to be known as the tax sale purchaser's substitute lien. There is a question about the priority of this lien, and whether it borrows or continues the state's super-priority position or has priority by when it was created as other liens commonly have.

...AN INVALID DEED DOES NOT CAUSE LOSS OF ALL INTEREST IN THE PROPERTY.

Recovery of the value of improvements made by the purchaser, who is later deprived of the property, is possible so long as any improvements were made after the one-year redemption period. § 140.360.2. In the case of any "planted, growing and/or unharvested crop on the lands" were placed after the one-year period but redeemed, the tax sale purchaser that planted such crops "shall be protected in the value" thereof. § 140.310.5.

The applicable statutes do not provide for carrying costs, other related transactional costs, or attorney fees, although in cases of equitable relief there may be common-law arguments to be made about entitlement to those forms of relief. *Williams v. Kimes*, 996 S.W.2d 43 (Mo. banc 1999).

If the collector discovers invalidity prior to deed issuance, they are not to issue the deed but instead refund the purchaser with interest. R.S.Mo. §§ 140.530 & 140.540.

Where taxes were paid prior to the sale, the purchaser's refund is taxes paid, plus interest, plus a ten percent penalty to the collector, to be paid out of the county commission. Where another reason causes invalidity (such as not liable for taxation when assessed, or more commonly inadequate legal description), the purchaser gets a refund with interest but without a penalty. The question of *exactly what interest rate* applies in these situations remains an unanswered question under Missouri law.

CHAPTER 19

NOTABLE DEVELOPMENTS AND CHANGES SINCE 2010

The Missouri Practice Series on Jones-Munger I first read was authored in 2010, appearing as Chapter 5 of the Real Estate Deskbook. The treatise is an excellent resource that has informed my practice. On more recent research, I found an update, 1 Mo. Real Estate Practice § 16.1-16.38 on Tax Sales (2019). It is a worthwhile read. The next section is more detail for the specialty practitioner, or the exceedingly curious (both of whom are *my* kind of people). These topics either arose, or arrived at my consciousness, after about 2010.

CHAPTER 20
SURPLUS BIDS

Surplusage occurs when there is competitive auction bidding[6] upon a desirable property. Surplus bids are tracked carefully and reported to the county clerk. If the property is redeemed, the surplus is returned to the purchaser without interest.

The surplus remains with the collector. If the property is redeemed, the surplus is paid back to the purchaser without interest. If the property is not redeemed, the purchaser gets a collector's deed. The surplus then becomes available for former owners or lienholders to claim, and the statute sets forth how to do this and who has priority.

The former statutory language said surplus was "to be held for the use and benefit of the person entitled to such moneys …". The statute got no more specific than that, and as you can surmise, it was not exactly a model of clarity. For years the "person entitled" was generally thought to be the former property owner, a consolation prize that helped close the gap between what the property was sold for and the fair market value. To the extent the sale represents the value of the property, the surplus is the homeowner's equity.

---

6   Or silent bidding, where other bids are unknown.

But "the person entitled to such moneys" could also be an heir if deceased, or perhaps a deed of trust grantee (mortgagee), a payment toward which debt would still help the former owner who lost their property. If the proper party did not claim it within three years, the money escheated to the county school fund.

In recent years, some tax sale purchasers started applying for the surplus or otherwise seeking to recover it through the courts. *See, e.g., summary judgment argument in Clay County, Missouri, et al. v. Anthony Morreale, et al.*, Clay County Case No. 14CY-CV09993, decided 2/29/16 (concluding the tax sale purchaser was not entitled to surplus). There were some situations where a mortgagee and a former owner both applied. In one instance, rumor has it that the former owner got the money and skipped town, leaving the mortgagee without recourse personally against their debtor, or *in rem* against the property. One might also suspect sustained low interest rates and rising property values created more incentives for surplus bidders seeking REO ("real estate owned").

As surpluses became more common, more attention was being paid to the issue. The lack of statutory direction as to how to deal with them led to bizarre arguments and unfair results.

A legislative amendment succeeded in 2018, creating a more defined and orderly surplus claim process. R.S.Mo. § 140.230. Now, there is a 90-day waiting period after the redemption period ends (the deed is recorded in favor of the tax sale purchaser). During that time, any owner or lienholder may file a formal written claim to the surplus, giving certain identifying information and supporting documentation.

Lienholders take priority over homeowners. If there are multiple lienholder claims, priority is determined by date order, as in most other lien priority situations. In other words, first in time, first in right, and that priority is determined as of the date of the tax sale – later encumbrances would yield no such entitlement. Owners, or their heirs, are in the next priority position. If there is a dispute about the claims and who should be paid what, the collector can interplead the money into court and be dismissed.

The statutory language seems to indicate no party other than a former owner or lien holder would be entitled to surplus funds. The amendment left unchanged the provision that surplus money escheats to the county school fund if no claims are made after three years.

...NO PARTY OTHER THAN A FORMER OWNER OR LIEN HOLDER WOULD BE ENTITLED TO SURPLUS FUNDS.

Claiming and procuring the surplus could be a ratification of the sale, and an estoppel to challenge it. *See* Chapter 13. Under this new process for claiming surpluses, it would be a different analysis if the former owner claimed but did not procure the surplus due to lower priority. In that case, it could be said the owner or lienholder never enjoyed the benefit of the sale, as they never received the money. But it could be argued the mere making of a claim to surplus is an acknowledgement of the sale's validity and an estoppel to challenge it. That case has not been made or decided under the new statute. At least not yet.

Additionally, surplus issues also need to be understood in light of *Tyler v. Hennepin County. See* Chapter 31.

CHAPTER 21

COLLECTOR DISCRETION

The statutes formerly indicated issuance and recording of a collector's deed was a ministerial function and required no discretion. This led to a certain confusion as to the collector's proper role in the process. Should they not review the collector's deed application and ensure the law is followed? If they notice a shortcoming, should they not take action? Are they not the last gatekeeper in ensuring the administrative foreclosure process is fairly applied, consistent with the statutes?

In the same 2013 legislative abrogation of the *Bosch* case discussed below, the legislature explicitly granted collectors discretion to review and approve deed applications. Most collectors are elected positions, so they are still accountable to the people via the next election, as well as to an abuse of discretion standard should they be challenged in court. Which is to say, this grant of discretion is not unfettered. But it does most likely take the thought of a writ of mandamus out of the realm of possible avenues of relief if the collector does not issue and record a deed after the tax sale purchaser has made its application. The statute now says the tax sale purchaser must comply with § 140.405 "to the satisfaction of the collector."

Tax sale purchasers at the time of the amendment feared this would create problems with deed issuance in certain counties, but those fears do not seem to have materialized in any significantly detrimental way. Nevertheless, a cooperative relationship with the collector is perhaps more important than ever.

CHAPTER 22

LEGISLATIVE ABROGATION OF *HARPAGON*

Harpagon MO, LLC v. Bosch, 370 S.W.3d 579 (Mo. banc 2012) and its companion case decided the same day, *Sneil v. Tybe Learning Center, Inc.*, 370 S.W.3d 562 (Mo. banc 2012), resolved a lower court split as to when a notice of the right to redeem had to be sent. Or perhaps more accurately, when a purchaser was "authorized to acquire a deed." A built-in flexibility that served collectors, tax sale purchasers, and delinquent taxpayers just fine was struck down by a narrow statutory interpretation of the Missouri Supreme Court.

The old way was that a tax sale purchaser could send their notices whenever they wanted, so long as they applied for the deed sometime after one year but before eighteen months (formerly 24 months).

The 2012 ruling in *Harpagon* said the notice was sent too late, for having been dispatched less than 90 days prior to the one-year anniversary of the sale. Ironically sending the notice "late" in this manner only gave the delinquent taxpayer *more* time to redeem.

After *Harpagon*, all notices had to be sent out at least 90 days prior to the one-year anniversary of the sale. This created some problems as to secondary notice efforts pursuant to due process, as well as timing of procuring and evaluating title search reports. It also created a problem as to the language of such a notice.

However, *Harpagon* and *Sneil* are no longer good law, at least as to their holdings that a notice of the right to redeem must be sent 90 days prior to the one-year anniversary of the tax sale. The legislature disliked the ruling and abrogated it during its very next session in 2013, by explicitly redefining when a purchaser is authorized to acquire the deed. *A.L. 2015 H.B. 613*. The new statutory language seems to revert us back to the thoughtful, workable analysis in *Boston v. Williamson*, 807 S.W.2d 216, 218 (Mo. App. W.D. 1991) and *United Asset Mgmt. Trust Co. v. Clark*, 332 S.W.3d 159 (Mo. App. W.D. 2010). Notices can be sent whenever, so long as they accurately describe redemption rights and are timed so as to hit the purchaser's window to get the deed – between one year and eighteen months after the sale.

Redemption notices generally state the existence of a right to redeem and the pendency of an action against the owner's interest, such that their rights may be forever foreclosed and barred if they do not act. As to timing, it must not indicate any shortening of either the absolute one-year period of redemption or the 90 days from the date the notice is sent. *United Asset* reiterated that it is probably acceptable to state a right to redeem is pending, and rather than describe it in detail. If the tax sale purchaser details the right,

REDEMPTION NOTICES STATE THE EXISTENCE OF A RIGHT TO REDEEM AND THE PENDENCY OF AN ACTION AGAINST THE OWNER'S INTEREST...

they must do so *correctly*, which is subject to interpretation. When something like this is subject to interpretation, that means it is subject to litigation. Litigation can be costly, such that even a win might be pyrrhic. Another option is simply to attach a copy of the applicable statute. *See* Chapter 15.

The statutory amendments and the case law from 2010 to current requires specialized focus to untangle. Close attention to the relevant dates of opinions and amendments is critical in understanding the trajectory of the law and where it sits currently.

CHAPTER 23

LOSS OF ONLY OWNERSHIP INTEREST FOR NON-COMPLIANCE

Formerly, § 140.405 tersely and unjustly provided that for certain non-compliance with notice provisions, the tax sale purchaser lost all interest in the property. Wisely, and consistent with the protection of the tax sale purchaser's investment, what is lost now is simply the *ownership* interest in the land. That is, the purchaser forfeits the right to get a deed, and instead is relegated to a lien. § 140.405.8, pursuant to §§ 140.405.8, 140.550, and 140.570 (2015). This is discussed prior in Chapter 6, as well, but is mentioned separately here as a notable development. The harsh language about loss of all interest only remains in § 140.440 regarding timely payment of subsequently due taxes.

CHAPTER 24

ADVERSE POSSESSION IN *YORK V. HORNER*

A third offering sale and resulting deed to a parcel of land was challenged by neighboring owners who claimed to own a strip of it by adverse possession. York was the tax sale purchaser, the Horners were the neighboring owners that constructed and maintained a concrete retaining wall on the strip. *York v. Horner*, 564 S.W.3d 641 (Mo. App. E.D. 2018). The court found only very old cases of inquiry notice prior to Jones-Munger, where a tax sale purchaser took subject to such an interest. The court did not find facts to support such a claim here, so as to fault the tax sale purchaser for failure to send notice to the challengers. Even if the Horners acquired a property interest by adverse possession, they still failed to pay taxes, and an unrecorded claim of adverse possession does not survive a tax sale. *Id. at 648.*

By contrast, an unrecorded easement may survive a tax sale, if it is "in use" pursuant to § 140.722. Under such circumstances, perhaps the "inquiry notice" cases cited in this opinion could be instructive.

The case also had an interesting footnote about a challenger's obligation to plead tender under § 140.600. The Court did not strike any defenses, but simply used the failure to tender to further distinguish the case factually from a prior case that went in favor of the challengers. *Adams v. Gossom*, 129 S.W. 16 (Mo. 1910).

CHAPTER 25

MERE IRREGULARITIES VERSUS AVAILABLE DEFENSES

The Missouri Eastern District Court of Appeals recently addressed the reconciliation of two seemingly conflicting tax sale statutes, § 140.190 and § 140.610. *WMAC 2013, LLC v. Dennie Gladney, et al.*, Case No. 16SL-CC04420, Appeal No. ED107204 (2020). The former statute states no sale *shall* be made to any person currently delinquent on any property other than the one offered for sale. The latter states in all suits or controversies a challenger *shall* be required to prove, in order to defeat the deed, certain defenses relating to the assessment and payment of taxes. Challenger homeowner argued tax sale purchaser failed to file an affidavit of non-delinquency as required by § 140.190, and tax sale purchaser argued that is not an available defense under § 140.610.

Respondent tax sale purchaser, who prevailed on summary judgment at the trial court, argued § 140.190 applies to a collector who *may* invalidate such a sale, and the "shall" therein is a grant of discretion to do so. At oral argument it was noted that the collector does not have blanket authority or unfettered discretion in banning a potential bidder or invalidating sales to a particular bidder. *Joel Yoest, et al. v. Lydia McEvoy*, 529 S.W.3d 383 (2017). Therefore a specific legislative grant of discretion to the collector to invalidate a sale for specific reasons was and is necessary.

In contrast, the tax sale purchaser argued, § 140.610 applies to suits or controversies, and is for the protection of the system as a whole. That is, § 140.190 governs day-of concerns, but once the sale is completed, the notices have been sent, the redemption period has lapsed, the deed was applied for, issued and recorded, and a quiet title suit seeks to confirm the title conveyed by said deed, there are much more limited means of challenging the sale. Only those considerations that go right to the heart of what a tax sale is all about are relevant in a quiet title lawsuit, and a sale should not be disturbed based on technicalities.

Whereas § 140.190 elucidates certain rights of collectors, § 140.610 addresses rights of title holders. There is no statutory language authorizing delinquent taxpayers to assert the collector's right to invalidate a sale for reasons outside § 140.610.

For failure to raise a genuine issue of material fact to rebut the *prima facie* case made by Plaintiff, summary judgment was affirmed. "Additionally, it bears noting that title-holders will only find themselves in this situation if they fail to pay their property taxes." *Id.* at 7. Application in Eastern District Court of Appeals for Transfer to the Missouri Supreme Court denied 2/18/20; Application in Missouri Supreme Court for Transfer to the Missouri Supreme Court denied 4/28/20.

CHAPTER 26
BETTERMENT STATUTE

In a recent case, a party closed on a loan over the certificate of purchase existing in county records and spent a substantial sum in renovating the property. In the quiet title following the collector's deed, the defendant filed a counterclaim to the ejectment action seeking to recover the value of improvements made to the property during the one-year redemption period.

The theory was pleaded pursuant to the betterment statute, R.S.Mo. § 524.160, which states:

> **524.160. Defendant may recover compensation for improvements, when.** — If a judgment or decree of dispossession shall be given in an action for the recovery of possession of premises, or in any real action in favor of a person having a better title thereto, against a person in the possession, held by himself or by his tenant, of any lands, tenements or hereditaments, such person may recover, in a court of competent jurisdiction, compensation for all improvements made by him in good faith on such lands, tenements or hereditaments, prior to his having had notice of such adverse title.

This type of claim raises a number of issues. First, it is of note that this statute embodies the common law and is based upon equitable notions. What it does not explicitly state in the statute, however, is that notice to the legal title holder also is required, else the statute is unconstitutional as applied. *See, e.g. First Federal Savings & Loan Assn. v. Wills*, 789 S.W.2d 873 (Mo. App. S.D. 1990); *Weatherwax v. Redding*, 953 S.W.2d 162 (Mo. App. S.D. 1997); *Morris v. Ulbright*, 591 S.W.2d 245 (Mo. App. W.D. 1979). So not only does an equitable improver have to prove good faith, but they must also show notice to the titled owner. This could be a high bar because it might entail even *actual* as opposed to merely *constructive* notice. If the titled owner has no knowledge of the improvements at the time they were being made, so as to have acquiesced in the improvements, there is no recourse. The legal title holder must have notice and an opportunity to object to the manner or method of improvements to his property, without which a judgment against him for the value of said improvements violates his due process rights.

AN EQUITABLE IMPROVER MUST PROVE GOOD FAITH, AND SHOW NOTICE TO THE TITLED OWNER.

Without the title holder's acquiescence in the improvements made, the improver has no recourse under common law or the statute. *Id.* That would result in a total loss of the value of improvements made. While the former owner may alternatively plead a count in unjust enrichment, they may have a similar problem, nonetheless. One of the elements of an unjust enrichment claim is knowledge or acceptance of the benefit conferred under unjust circumstances.

The only remedy may be a claim to their title insurance, and that depends on the terms of their policy.

CHAPTER 27

FORECLOSURE SALES CONDUCTED IN THE SAME MANNER AS TAX SALES

Certain other statutes in Missouri provide for the foreclosure of liens in the same manner as tax liens.

In *Real Estate Recovery, LLC v. Branson Hills Facility Infrastructure Community Improvement District*, 614 S.W.3d 541 (Mo. App. S.D. 2020), the Southern District addressed the extinguishment or survival of community improvement district assessments following a Community Improvement District ("CID") foreclosure sale that was conducted in the same manner as a post-third offering tax sale.

First, we should discuss what this case is not. It is not a tax sale case. The parcels involved here were sold for *assessments*, not for *taxes*. Further, it is not a case distinguishing between assessments and installments due on a previous assessment, as in *Suncrest*. *Branson Hills* does not address the survival of past assessments or intervening assessments (those assessments made post-sale but prior to the recording of a deed). And because this was a Community Improvement District case, it does not specifically address assessments or installments due on assessments from a Transportation Development District, a Neighborhood Improvement District, or any such similar type of interest or lien.

Nevertheless, *Branson Hills* has relevant analysis to tax sale jurisprudence. The Court stated, the "sole and *narrow* issue before us is whether – in light of the controlling provisions of the CID Act and the Jones-Munger Act – assessments levied or imposed by the District against the parcels after the post-third offering sale survive, [so] as to impose a continuing lien on the parcels (and corresponding obligation on Real Estate Recovery to remit payment for such subsequently levied or imposed assessments)."

Siding with the CID assessments surviving the foreclosure sale conducted in the same manner as a tax sale, the Court stated there is an orderly process in the CID statute for terminating a CID, and to allow a collector's deed grantee to extricate the property from the district creates a "free-riding" problem as to future assessments made. The *Branson Hills* court arrived at this conclusion for two primary reasons: (1) to the extent Jones-Munger and the CID Act conflict as to whether a CID assessment survives, in this case the CID controlled because this was not a tax sale authorized by Jones-Munger, but a CID foreclosure sale conducted in the same manner as a tax sale, authorized by the CID Act, and (2) because the CID statute included reference to each assessment being a "perpetual lien" as stated in the CID Act, R.S.Mo. § 67.1401 et seq.

Clearly, the Missouri Courts believe the legislature has the power and discretion to elevate lien priorities to be on par with taxes. But that analysis plainly leaves, for another day, a lien or other interest created by a different act, such as TDD or NID, as to whether or how the legislature has done that within each respective elevating statute. *See non-exhaustive list herein, fn. 8; accord § 249.255 sewer district liens,* Chapter 26. This is a developing area of the law.

CHAPTER 28
SEWER DISTRICT LIENS

Missouri has three separate statutes allowing for the creation of sewer districts. The biggest such district seems to be The Metropolitan St. Louis Sewer District ("MSD"), https://msdprojectclear.org/. MSD states as the reason for their creation, "From 1835 through 1850, the St. Louis population grew by 425%. Due to overcrowding and lack of sanitation, cholera spread throughout the city culminating in an 1849 epidemic killing nearly 5,000 people. In the 1850s, city leaders began developing a combined sanitary and wastewater sewer system, portions of which are still in use today." Others exist around the eastern and southern parts of the state. *See, e.g.,* http://www.moasd.com/Missouri-Association-Sewer-District-Members.asp.

In a recent surprise to many industry participants, a Missouri court recently held that even *unrecorded* sewer liens are not extinguished by a Missouri tax sale, making a tax sale purchaser's land liable for all outstanding sewer bills. *Eclipse Property Development LLC v. Fareed Ammari, et al.,* ED109298 (2021), *motion for rehearing or transfer denied 10/28/21* (dealing not with MSD, but Northeast Public Sewer District). The *Eclipse* Court stated the legislature has the power to change priorities of liens and give statutory liens priority over others, and further that as to sewer district liens, R.S.Mo. § 249.255 does just that. [7]

While tax liens are superior to all others, the *Eclipse* Court held § 249.255 makes unpaid sewer charge liens of equal priority. The statutory language was adopted in 2000, applicable only to sewer districts within St. Louis County, states:

> Should a public sewer district created and organized pursuant to constitutional or statutory authority place a lien upon a customer's property for unpaid sewer charges, the lien shall have priority as and be enforced in the same manner as taxes levied for state and county purposes.

In *Eclipse*, the sewer district only placed a lien after the sale, but the Court saw that as irrelevant because they were not subject to the typical first-in-time-first-in-right priority rules, as the statute gives them equal priority.

But does that not mean the Court made sewer district charges *superior* to taxes? That is, if priorities are equal, should the holders of those equal-priority liens not share pro rata (*"pari passu"*) in foreclosure proceeds?

The Eastern District does not think so. Rather, they state, "[t]he general rule is that the lien of special tax bills for local improvements is inferior to that of general taxes **where there is no provision to the contrary."** *Id., citing Associated Holding*

---

7   Eclipse was a Jefferson County case, regarding a Jefferson County property, 2909 High Ridge Blvd., High Ridge MO 63049. R.S.Mo. §249.255 regards only St. Louis County sewer liens. Yet the Court cites to this statute 29 times in its opinion. It seems everyone missed this point. But it may be a distinction without a difference: R.S.Mo. § 249.640.2 (adopted 1941, most recently amended in 1983), relating to sewer districts in "Other Counties," has identical language.

Co. v. Carrigg, 65 S.W.2d 1059, 1060 (Mo. App. K.C.D. 1933). Because § 249.255 changes the priority of St. Louis County sewer charge liens, the same could not be extinguished by a tax sale.

Thereafter the Court sympathizes that the tax sale purchaser had no notice. The Court says the purchaser was a bona fide purchaser, but apparently believes everyone is on constructive notice of sewer charge priority. If they were not prior, they are now, at least.

The reasoning here is critical for future cases in other contexts, such as TDD or NID. Neither the TDD Act nor the NID Act provide elevated lien priority. Therefore, by negative implication, those interests would be inferior to the priority of liens for general taxes, and thus extinguishable at a tax sale. Though that case is yet to be decided.

It would stand to reason that the statute must not only discuss *collection* in the same manner as taxes, but specifically provide for *priority* in the same manner as taxes in order for such a lien to survive a tax sale. Clearly the legislature knows how to use that language, if it so intends.

In addition, recall the language in § 249.255.1 has two parts: (1) priority as taxes, and (2) enforcement in the same manner as taxes. *Eclipse* addresses the first part, but not the second. There is little definition to what it means to be collected in the same manner as taxes – do *all* provisions for collecting or prioritizing taxes now apply to these otherwise-inferior liens? An interesting question, for example, is the limitations period for lien enforcement and expiration.

A diligent tax sale purchaser would check if a property they want to bid upon is within a sewer district and what, if any, charges are outstanding. Their purchase in St. Louis County (and likely all other counties) is almost certainly subject to those charges, and they are on notice. For other types of liens, one would need to consult the district's or other interest-holder's authorizing or governing statute to determine if the legislature changed lien priorities.

A DILIGENT TAX SALE PURCHASER WOULD CHECK IF A PROPERTY THEY WANT TO BID UPON IS WITHIN A SEWER DISTRICT...

CHAPTER 29

ATTORNEY FEES AS A RECOVERABLE COST UPON REDEMPTION

The Missouri statute governing recoverable costs upon redemption is § 140.340.2:

The reasonable and customary costs of sale include **all** costs incurred in selling and foreclosing tax liens under this chapter, and such reasonable and customary costs shall include the following: the full sum of the purchase money named in the certificate of purchase and all the costs of the sale, including the cost to record the certificate of purchase as required in section 140.290, the fee necessary for the collector to record the release of such certificate of purchase, and the reasonable and customary cost of the title search and postage costs of notification required in sections 140.150 to 140.405, together with interest at the rate specified in such certificate, not to exceed ten percent annually, except on a sum paid by a purchaser in excess of the delinquent taxes due plus costs of the sale incurred by the collector, no interest shall be owing on the excess amount, with all subsequent taxes which have been paid thereon by the purchaser, his or her heirs or assigns with interest at the rate of eight percent per annum on such taxes subsequently paid, and in addition thereto the person redeeming any land shall pay the costs incident to entry of recital of such redemption; provided, however, that no costs incurred by tax sale purchasers in providing notice of tax sale redemption rights required by law shall be reimbursable as a reasonable and customary cost of sale unless such costs are incurred after March first following the date of purchase of the tax sale certificate by said tax sale purchaser at a first or second offering delinquent tax sale. (emphasis added)

Payment of such costs is a condition of redemption. The tax sale purchaser reports such costs, and the collector is the arbiter of reasonable and customary. § 140.340.5.

Because, as discussed above, tax sales are governed both by statute and due process, often an attorney assists tax sale purchasers in determining who is entitled to notice, where notices should be sent, what notices should say, and what, if any, follow up attempts are necessary to meet the dictates of these two sources of governing law. Attorney fees are not listed as a customary cost, but is the list in § 140.340.2 exhaustive or illustrative?

The list is illustrative and attorney fees, therefore, are a "potentially reimbursable" cost of redemption. So the Court held in *Missouri Bond Company, LLC v. Mark R. Devore, et al.*, ED109475, (Mo. App. E.D. 2/15/22). The tax sale purchaser sought attorney fees as a recoverable cost upon redemption,

"YOU CAN NEVER GIVE TOO MUCH NOTICE; YOU CAN ONLY GIVE TOO LITTLE..."

noting: "You can never give too much notice; you can only give too little – and you only find out you gave too little notice after a court tells you so, and it is too late to fix the problem."

The Court stated the tax sale purchaser is required to (1) submit invoices clearly identifying each category of cost, and (2) establish each cost as reasonable and customary. That submission triggers the Collector's duty to assess the reasonable and customary nature of each such category of costs. On judicial review, the court will consider both parties' actions in this respect and weigh these factors: (1) complicated nature of the title search, (2) multiple property owners [or presumably lienholders], (3) various years of unpaid taxes, (4) computation of interest, and (5) drafting and filing of necessary documents to effectuate a clear transfer of title. *Id.* The case was remanded, and later dismissed, so this area remains under development.

CHAPTER 30

AMENDMENTS FOR ONLINE AUCTIONS

House Bill 1606 successfully added the following sentence at the end of § 140.170.3: "**Such auction may also be conducted by electronic media, including the internet, at the same time and at the discretion of the county collector.**" The same bill made a corresponding change to § 140.190.2 (in bold): "The person or land bank agency offering at said sale, **whether in person or by electronic media,** to pay the required sum for a tract shall be considered the purchaser of such land …" The bill was part of an omnibus bill and appears to be a simple effort toward recognizing the modernization of the process. As some collectors already were conducting online sales, this simply clarifies their discretion to do so. H.B. 1606 was truly agreed and finally passed 5/11/22, signed by Governor Parson 6/29/22, and took effect 8/28/22.

But also note, that bill was later declared unconstitutional in violation of the single subject rule of Article III, Section 23 of the Missouri Constitution. *See Byrd, et al. v. State of Missouri, et al.,* SC100045 (Mo. banc 12/19/23) (H.B. 1606 declared invalid in its entirety). This case does not seem to have had an impact in deterring online sales.

CHAPTER 31
FEDERAL LIENS

In Show Me State Premium Homes v. McDonnell, 4:21-CV-00379-SEP (U.S. Dist. Ct., E.D. Mo., Hon. Judge Pitlyk, 3/31/22) (8th Cir. App. Case No. 22-1894), the trial court held that a HUD lien belonging to the federal government was not extinguished by a tax sale because 28 U.S.C. § 2410(c) only allows extinguishment of federal liens following a *judicial* sale but not a *non-judicial* foreclosure sale such as in Missouri's Jones-Munger Act.[8]

The 8th Circuit affirmed *per curiam* 7/20/23. In footnotes 2 and 3 of the opinion, however, the holding is expressly limited to judicial foreclosure actions under 28 U.S.C. § 2410(a)(2), finding that the Plaintiff/Appellant "insisted throughout that it sought title through foreclosure and, until oral argument, never argued otherwise." In essence, the Court declined to analyze sovereign immunity waiver under any of the other types of civil actions under 28 U.S.C. § 2410(a), including quiet title actions.

Because Missouri's tax sale process is administrative, it was not a judicial sale. And it was too late to hold a judicial

---

8   Except for IRS liens, which are expressly subordinated to state tax liens under 26 U.S.C. § 7425(b).

sale after the deed recording because SMSPH owns the property. Therefore, the trial court was without power to assess whether or not the HUD interest was foreclosed (even though the opinion overstates that the HUD lien was not foreclosed).

The Missouri process could still be sufficient to both foreclose a federal lien administratively and confirm the same in a traditional quiet title action. However, the tax sale purchaser will have to be careful on how it pleads for relief such that it falls under 28 U.S.C. § 2410(a)(1) instead of 28 U.S.C. § 2410(a)(2). I remain of the belief that 28 U.S.C. § 2410(c)'s judicial sale requirement applies only to 28 U.S.C. § 2410(a)(2).

For greater detail on this argument, find the oral argument audio here: https://www.ca8.uscourts.gov/case-number-0, enter Case No. 22-1894, click "MP3" link on the far right. The argument traces the history and current language of the Federal Tax Lien Act of 1966, *U.S. v. Brosnan*, 363 U.S. 237 (1960), & *U.S. v. Kimbell Foods*, 400 U.S. 715 (1979). See also motion for panel rehearing in 22-1894, filed 8/18/23, denied 9/12/23. Future cases on this issue seem inevitable, though not necessarily immediate.

CHAPTER 32

US SUPREME COURT DECIDES 8TH CIRCUIT TAX SALE CASE

Attorneys and tax sale industry participants closely watched the development of _Tyler v. Hennepin County, Minnesota, et al._, United States Supreme Court Docket No. 22-166 (argued 4/26/23; decided 5/25/23). A Minnesota grandmother's condo was foreclosed for $15,000 in taxes. Minnesota law provides a period of time prior to forfeiture where the owner can sell the property, pay their tax debt, and retain the equity from the sale. Tyler did not do so.

Hennepin County came into ownership of the condo and state law provided no method for Tyler to claim the surplus or equity.[9] Hennepin County later sold the condo for $45,000 and kept the profit.

Appellant argued an unconstitutional taking without adequate compensation, as well as an excessive fine, both in violation of the US Constitution as applied to the States via the 14th Amendment. The National Tax Lien Association, NTLA,

---

9   Apparently 26 other states have a similar foreclosure process.

filed an amicus brief 3/31/23 (among numerous other amici) urging the Court to allow states to determine the procedures of their own tax sales.

In a 9-0 decision, the court found Tyler's claims survive a motion to dismiss as stating claims for unconstitutional taking without just compensation. The Court seemed to indicate that some procedure to claim the surplus or equity would have saved the Minnesota law and brought it within constitutional confines. Justice Roberts, who wrote the majority opinion, rejected outright the argument that allowing a private sale prior to the taking is a sufficient substitute for some procedure to claim the surplus or equity after the taking. The Court also summarily rejected the argument that Tyler had constructively abandoned her property, saying there is no authority that failure to pay real estate taxes alone is enough to find the required present intent to abandon. "The taxpayer must render to Caesar what is Caesar's, but no more." *At p. 14.*

Gorsuch and Jackson concurred and would have found in addition to the Court's majority holding, that the Minnesota statutory scheme also violated the constitution's excessive fines clause.

I believe that states providing for a public auction and some method of recovering tax sale surpluses, such as Missouri, are significantly distinguishable. But how much further the Court is willing to go and how much procedure is enough to be constitutional are unanswered questions almost certain to be litigated in the coming years and decades.

Challenges could arise here in Missouri following the Court's opinion in this case. Rumor has it other states more similar to Minnesota will be targeted next.

CHAPTER 33

MISSOURI TAX SALE SEMINAR

If you want to know more about Missouri tax sales, regardless of your perspective or participation in the industry, Missouri Tax Sale Seminar, LLC presents a very affordable annual conference on the subject. The seminar qualifies for Continuing Legal Education credit for Missouri attorneys. The first annual Missouri Tax Sale Seminar was Friday, 6/17/22 in Columbia MO and via Zoom, with approximately 60 in attendance. MTSS 2 was Friday, 6/2/23 in St. Louis MO, with approximately 80 in attendance. MTSS 3 will be Friday 6/21/24 in Gladstone MO and via Zoom. All information and the registration form are available at:

www.mtss.llc

The seminar is presented by Missouri Tax Sale Seminar, LLC, organized by me in Fall 2021. For more information email scott@mtss.llc.

CHAPTER 34

CONCLUSION

As a first year law student, I was told law school was much like a game of chess. You spent the semester learning all the rules. Then you sit down to take the final exam as if you are sitting down to play the game for the first time. Many are overwhelmed at the prospect as was I, but I persevered.

In the subsequent semesters, I figured out the game. I understood better what it took to prepare. I understood the themes and arcs of each class. I spent a few semesters on the Dean's List.

Knowing some of the rules is helpful, in fact necessary, for the players and spectators in tax sales. I've been in the tax sale arena for many years, striving, developing, striving differently, being humbled, and striving again. It is my hope this book brings you a little closer to the arena, to see the complexity, appreciate the different perspectives, and understand all the stakeholders.

I hope this book looks good on the shelf and is a reference point for you, as it already has been for me.

Relationships, risk, balance, and gratitude always. Cheers, friends.

mtss

missouri tax sale seminar, llc

Kansas City, MO

scott@mtss.llc | 816-601-1100

www.mtss.llc

WA